Primer for Protestants

Haddam House

HADDAM HOUSE is a publishing project in the field of religious literature for youth. Its special concern is the moral and religious questions and needs of young men and women. It gathers up and continues the interests that led to the publication of the Hazen Books on Religion and is directed primarily to students and employed young people.

HADDAM HOUSE seeks as authors new voices qualified to give fresh guidance to thoughtful youth. In consultation with leaders of the United Student Christian Council and other groups, HADDAM HOUSE is studying the changing needs for literature in its field and developing methods of wide distribution.

Policy and program for HADDAM HOUSE are under the direction of an Editorial Board which represents common concerns of the Edward W. Hazen Foundation, Woman's Press, and Association Press, together with educators and religious leaders from various Christian churches and agencies. At present the Editorial Board includes: Paul M. Limbert, Chairman; Edwin E. Aubrey; John C. Bennett; Virginia Corwin; Grace Loucks Elliott; Lawrence K. Hall; William Hubben; Harold B. Ingalls; Paul L. Lehmann; John Oliver Nelson; J. Edward Sproul; Rose Terlin; Paul Braisted.

PRIMER FOR PROTESTANTS

By James Hastings Nichols

A HADDAM HOUSE BOOK

ASSOCIATION PRESS—NEW YORK—1947

145

PRINTED IN THE UNITED STATES OF AMERICA

Contents

༤༤༤༤༤༤༤༤༤༤༤༤༤༤༤༤༤༤༤༤༤༤༤༤༤༤༤༤༤༤༤༤༤༤༤༤༤༤

PART 2. PROTESTANT PRINCIPLES

Introduction

∿∿

THE DEFINITION OF PROTESTANTISM presents two sides.
The actual Protestant churches that we know came into existence, for the most part, in the period of the Reformation,
the sixteenth and seventeenth centuries. They organized as
separate churches in a mood of complete disillusionment
with the existing Roman Catholic church organization. And
there remains in Protestantism this memory of a solemn
repudiation, of death and rebirth. One important half of the
truth, consequently, locates the origins of Protestantism in
the Reformation, and defines it by contrast to Roman Catholicism. As Bishop Dun puts it, all Christians are naturally
Catholic until they learn by bitter experience to be something
better. And the commonest meaning of the word "Protestant" today in Western countries is simply, "any Christian
who denies the authority of the Roman pope."

But if only this half of the truth is seen, Protestantism is
quite misconceived. To the taunt, "Where was your church
before the Reformation?" an Anglican replied shrewdly if
somewhat inelegantly, "Where was your face before you
washed it this morning?" Protestantism also represents a
genuine revival of the life and gospel of the apostles, and
even a continuation of certain major streams of religious life
of the Latin middle ages. On several important issues Protestantism is in the main line of Western Christian history
and it is modern Romanism which represents the innovation
and "protest." Modern Roman Catholicism was radically
reorganized in creed, government, and worship in reaction
to the Reformation, and is historically incomprehensible save
as a protest against Protestantism. Many peripheral aspects

7

of the life of the undivided church which the Reformation
had attacked or belittled were now deliberately moved into
the center of emphasis and many novelties established. A
new denomination was created, as "Protestant" in the negative sense as Lutheranism or Calvinism, and yet like them
having also certain roots and precedents in the undivided
church. Modern Romanism and modern Protestantism alike
are partly revolutionary and partly traditional and neither
can be fully understood without relating it to the other.

American Protestants, however, have somewhat lost the
consciousness of their peculiarities as Protestants. This is
partly due to the fact that until this generation American
culture has been so pervasively and unexceptionably Protestant that Americans have come to take their Protestant
heritage as a matter of course. As André Siegfried wrote,
Protestantism is America's "only national religion, and to
ignore that fact is to view the country from a false angle."
Protestants will now become more self-conscious, however,
as they learn increasingly what the character of Roman
Catholicism is. This is a somewhat startling experience to
many Americans. Roman Catholicism had practically no
influence on American constitution or culture through the
19th century. As late as the first World War half the Roman
Catholics in America were still in foreign language churches
and Roman Catholics generally felt themselves an alien colony among "the Americans." It was only a generation ago
that the United States ceased officially to be a Roman mission
field. While the cessation of immigration has ended the
period of Roman Catholic growth, and probably stabilized
them indefinitely at about a sixth of the population, in this
present generation the Roman Catholic hierarchy at last feels
strong enough to promote aggressively those views which
challenge sharply the American Protestant heritage and
which are stimulating the latter to new self-consciousness.

There remains nearly one third of Christendom which is

organized in the churches which proudly call themselves "Orthodox," the eastern churches of the Balkans, Russia and Asia Minor. They are neither Protestant nor Roman Catholic, but have a distinctive character of their own, in some ways more resembling the one, and in others the other. With them should also be grouped a variety of other "Catholics" who do not obey the pope, Anglo-Catholics, Old Catholics, Polish National Catholics, Brazilian Catholics. We must seek to define the relationship of Protestantism to this family of churches as well as to Roman Catholicism.

There is no use arguing over words, and life is too short to campaign against incorrect usage. A word of regret may be expressed, nevertheless, at that partiality of popular usage which has accorded in the modern English-speaking world the grand old word "catholic"—universal—to the Roman communion, while to that great company stemming institutionally from the Reformation it attaches the term "Protestant." No doubt few understand what either signifies, but a first inquiry would seem to indicate that "catholic" indicates something of significance and value, something too big for Romanism in fact, while "Protestant" seems to represent a residue without positive significance, equivalent to "non-Roman Catholic, miscellaneous."

The emptiness of the term "Protestant" is in large measure the outcome of a curious inversion of the meaning of the word "protest" since Elizabethan days. "Protestant" to Elizabethan Englishmen did not signify an objector, but rather one who bore a witness, who made an avowal. The contemporary "Confessing Church" of the German resistance has caught again the original significance of "Protestantism" in the English-speaking world, as a testifying church, a witnessing church. This was the connotation which made suitable the adoption of the term "Protestant." Originally the term referred, no doubt, to an appeal in the German diet of 1529 to "states' rights" and a previously agreed-on gen-

eral church council. This incident of the second decade of
the German Reformation, with its appeal to constitutional
procedure, was not primary in the English adoption of the
term. From the days of Elizabeth the English Protestant
church was the church which bore its witness and made its
avowal of evangelical Christianity in the Thirty-nine Articles.
Puritans, Presbyterians, and other critics of this confessing
church were not recognized in England as themselves "Protestant" until after the middle of the seventeenth century.
Only after the word "protest" changed its emphasis from
the positive to the negative sense in general use did the term
"Protestant" come to include all dissent from Romanism,
whatever its positive avowal.

Outside English-speaking lands the sons of the Reformation have not been betrayed in this way by the natural evolution of language. On the Continent and in Latin America
the terms "evangelicals" or "reformed" are generally used,
the one sometimes applied more particularly to the Lutheran
and the other to the Calvinist wings of the Reformation tradition. Neither term, with all the special connotations it
may have acquired, suffers from such serious disadvantages
as a title for the sum-product of the Reformation as does the
word now irretrievably established in English usage and in
general misunderstanding. "Evangelicalism" expresses best
the positive message to which early "Protestants" were witnessing, the good news of healing in Christ's Kingdom. A
less ambiguous title for this book would thus be "a primer
of evangelical Christianity," and when the word Protestant
is used, it signifies, not everything non-Roman and non-
Eastern Orthodox, but *evangelical* Protestantism, the Protestantism born of and living by a witness to the full and
revivified gospel.

We do not undertake to describe groups which are not in
this sense evangelicals. Yet the line cannot be clearly drawn
in terms of denominations. The American Unitarians, for

example, include some folk who vehemently do not believe in God, to say nothing of Jesus Christ. Other Unitarians are evangelicals in the tradition of Channing and Martineau. The same distinction is to be observed even within some denominations belonging to the Federal Council. This difficulty of drawing the line on the institutional map in no way decreases its fundamental importance in the nature of things and for this discussion.

We shall begin with a survey of the unbroken life of the evangelical fellowship from the days of the apostles to our own, and proceed to a definition of certain principles of Protestant life and thought. In this statement of evangelical faith, as with all Protestant statements, we shall be testifying to the experience of the fellowship, in this case of many living and many dead, but with no notion of finality or adequacy. This statement lies under the correction of the unending dialogue of the evangelical community with the God who makes himself known there, and will have served its purpose if it brings someone into that fellowship and to the hearing of the speaking God.

Part 1

The Protestant Movement

Chapter I

Origins: Eastern Orthodox and Evangelical

ᘛᘛᘛ

Protestant Unity and Diversity

THE MOST FAMILIAR THEME of critics of Protestantism is its .divisiveness. Each succeeding religious census in the United States turns up a few more startlingly named "store-front churches." We are now about the three hundred mark, and old Bossuet's theme of the infinite divisiveness of Protestantism seems amply justified by its ongoing history. Yet we should not be hasty. A second look at the census discloses that this vast proliferation of sects really involves only a very small proportion of people who for largely sociological reasons do not feel at home in the better established churches. A few of the sects grow and become in time assimilated to the main stream of Protestant Christianity, but the great majority last but a few years and are replaced by other equally ephemeral organizations. It will enable us to keep some hold on reality to remember that 90 per cent of the church members of America are found within twenty denominations, and over 80 per cent within thirteen denominations. The vast shifting phantasmagoria of Pentecostals, Assemblies of God, and the like, account for only one-tenth of church people with nine-tenths of the denominations. And while there is an indefinite margin of sects shading off outside Christianity altogether into astrology, spiritualism, theosophy, and the like, the main body of sects falls into one recognizable type of Protestantism and can be analyzed without too great distortion as America's twenty-

15

first denomination. Twenty-one is still a large number, but it does not stagger the imagination, nor preclude comparative study. We may even be permitted a further reduction; more than four out of five American Protestants belong to one of the six great families of Protestant churches: Baptist and Disciples, Methodist, Lutheran, Anglican and Episcopalian, Presbyterian and Reformed, Congregational-Christian. These same six families include nine-tenths of the Protestants in the rest of the world. We do not mean to underrate the richness and variety of Protestantism, nor the full claim of smaller groups to the name of evangelical Protestantism, nor the fact that there is not nearly enough co-operation and consolidation within Protestantism. These things are all important truths. What is not sufficiently recognized, however, is the fact that behind the perennially prolific frontier of organizational Protestantism, the main body has displayed a remarkable institutional stability.

Far more important than numerical considerations in these matters is the inner meaning of this complicated organization of Protestantism. Romanists often criticize Protestant divisions with the too hasty assumption that Protestant denominations are all sects in the sense that Roman Catholicism is a sect. This is, on the whole, not true. One can find Protestant denominations who maintain, like Rome, that they alone are the true church. Certain Lutheran, Baptist, and "holiness" groups come to mind. For the great majority of Protestants, however, the denominational structure is only an administrative differentiation within a common faith. Methodists, Presbyterians, Congregationalists, for example, who have actually united in Canada, generally regard each other as equally Christian, and their rivalry is no more serious than that between Jesuits and Dominicans, Benedictines and Redemptorists, Irish Catholics and German Catholics, the followers of Maritain and Sturzo and the supporters of Franco and the Inquisition. The Roman Catholics have a

central agency which can at least force silence when the
dissensions of various Romanist traditions or national organizations become too hot, but one may seriously doubt whether
the suspension of central discipline would disclose one degree
more of real trust and fellowship within the Roman communion than exists within Protestantism. The difference
between the two great communions is that Protestants wash
their dirty linen in public. The method leads to greater
scandal and inefficiency, but avoids, on the other hand, the
intrigue, tattle-telling and hypocrisy which corrode the relationships of Roman Catholics.

As we seek to describe the characteristic emphasis of each
of the main traditions of Protestantism, we find a bewilder-
ing flexibility and variety. There is an extraordinary richness
of religious temperament — mystical, ethical, rationalist,
Biblicist, even sacramentalist — organized now in state
churches with a sense of responsibility for all culture, now
in world-renouncing celibate colonies of monastics, or again
in an indefinite variety of types in between. Protestantism
exhibits a comprehensive and catholic life in contrast to the
narrow and doctrinaire character the Council of Trent imposed on modern Romanism. The spaciousness and color
of the undivided Latin church of the fifteenth century have
found a more adequate continuation in the communions
which retained fifteenth century constitutionalism than in
that which further sharpened centralized absolutism. Protestant unity can never consist in uniformity.

But even uniformity has been an ideal of much of Protestantism for much of its history. This conception, in fact,
provides us with the most convenient key to the confusing
history of Protestant institutions. The movements of the
Reformation may be divided into two groups, a conservative
group which retained the medieval conception of a uniform,
church-dominated state and culture, and a liberal wing, often
persecuted, which continued rather the medieval traditions

of separatist congregational life or of individualist humanists
or mystics. The former group produced the three great
ecclesiastical systems of the sixteenth and seventeenth centuries, the Lutheran state-churches of Germany and Scandinavia, the Anglican church, and the Reformed churches
of Switzerland, Holland, France, Scotland, and New England. Together with the new Romanism of Spain, Italy,
France, and east-central Europe these three great ecclesiastical
cultures constituted a renewal of the medieval ideal for two
centuries, as it were four medievalisms living side by side,
in debate and often in war. All claimed to rest on the dogmatic tradition of the ancient church and all rejected Copernicus and Galileo. All rejected also, with even greater severity
than had the later middle ages, the religious groups which
gave up the ideal of uniformity. Romanists, Calvinists,
Lutherans, Anglicans found an ominous convergence of purpose in the savage persecution of separatist sects and rationalistic and mystical individualists, the humanistic and
"Anabaptist" movements. We may thus distinguish three
varieties of authoritarian Protestantism and two general tendencies of a non-authoritarian Protestantism in the first two
centuries of our history.

The end of the seventeenth century, however, marked a
tremendous revolution in the relation of European culture
and states to Christianity. The savage and sterile wars of religion in France, Holland, Germany, England, and Scotland
convinced the groups directing these states that the authoritarian, religiously uniform society was no longer possible.
Roman Catholicism has never accepted this judgment of
history as final and still dreams of a "Roman Catholic state,"
even for the United States of America. All of the three great
Protestant medievalisms, on the other hand, accepted the
judgment, slowly, regretfully, imperfectly, but finally. And as
the pressure of persecution eased, the two suppressed Protestant tendencies, the humanist and mystical, and the separatist congregationalists, enjoyed *their* Reformation. The

triumph of this free Protestantism did not so much produce new denominations and movements, although some such appeared, like the Methodists, as it captured the thought and life of the formerly uniform churches. Humanist, rationalist, and mystical tendencies established themselves as important and sometimes dominant streams in the theology of Lutherans, Anglicans, and Calvinists in the eighteenth and nineteenth centuries. The Anabaptist conception of the separation of the church from the state profoundly changed the thinking even of churches which remained nominally state churches, while such churches experienced a penetration of voluntary fellowships of the Anabaptist type *within* their inherited structure. One result has been that modern Lutherans and Presbyterians, for example, to say nothing of Anglicans, often find themselves more congenial to men like Erasmus or Servetus or Sebastian Franck than they do to those founders from whom they stem. As Harnack wrote of some of the Anabaptist leaders who were fiercely attacked by the great Reformers, "many of these noble and reverend characters come nearer to us than the figures of an heroic Luther and an iron Calvin." Thus the minor and suppressed strains of the Reformation have come to be those most characteristic of modern Protestantism. It is this internal revolution, together with ever-increasing mutual borrowings down the generations, and the common inheritance of evangelical Christianity down to the Reformation, that makes it possible and indeed necessary to treat Protestantism as a whole, even if a whole composed of diverse tendencies in continual tension and fruitful debate.

The Church of the Martyrs

Before we proceed to analyze further these conservative and liberal tendencies of the Reformation, and their relation to the six great families of contemporary Protestantism, we should glance briefly at the tradition from which they came and to which they appealed. They all harked back from the shame into which the church had sunk in the sixteenth century to earlier and more glorious epochs. And the particular epochs idealized by the several groups are highly characteristic. Just as the politically ambitious Roman Catholic dreamed of the thirteenth century as the "century of faith," so the Anglican and Orthodox Catholic preferred the ancient church of the Roman Empire of the fourth and fifth centuries with its bishops, sacraments, and creeds, but as yet without a sovereign pope. Lutherans and Calvinists, like Anglicans, honored the creeds of the ancient councils but their hearts leaped up at the gospel preached by Paul in the first, and revived by Augustine in the fifth, century. The more radical wing likewise turned to the first century, back past all the centuries of great ecclesiastical organizations, to acclaim the liberty and independence of the primitive Christian communities. Mystics found deep things in the fourth gospel, rigorous moralists quoted the Sermon on the Mount, and millenarians pored over the allegories of the end of the world in Revelation. Certain Baptists in the United States are rumored to claim a genealogy older than "Protestants" and "Catholics" alike, deriving themselves from Jesus' predecessor John.

The very notion of an enduring community down the ages, had, of course, no place in the thought of Jesus. He sent messengers to preach the news that the Reign of God was at hand, and apparently felt that there was scarcely time to reach the tribes of Israel. There was neither time nor purpose for a settled institution, and as for government among his followers, James and John were rebuked for asking for some of the prerogatives later claimed by the bishops of Rome. Jesus gathered the men who were to minister in the church, but its birthday came after his resurrection, at Pentecost. It was the risen Christ, not the mortal Jesus, who laid on the disciples the injunction to preach to all nations, and this leading of his Spirit was only gradually accepted by them, as Paul's struggles demonstrate.

Paul, the great missionary to the non-Jewish world, first discussed the nature of this new creation, the church. The church was to continue the labor of Jesus, preaching the Kingdom and actually bringing it by mediating God's forgiveness and reconciliation. She was defined, consequently, as a second incarnation, a body whose indwelling spirit is that of the resurrected Christ. There are two characteristics of this continuing apostolate of the Kingdom, the extraordinary mutuality and fellowship which comes from the constant ministry one to another of God's forgiveness, and the continual sense of dependence on the spirit of Christ. "As the human body is one and has many members, all the members of the body forming one body for all their number, so is it with Christ. For by one Spirit we have all been baptized into one Body, Jews or Greeks, slaves or freemen . . . thus, if one member suffers, all the members share its suffering; if one member is honored, all the members share its honor." Through all the scattered brotherhoods in the cities of Asia Minor, Europe, and Africa there was this vivid sense of being *one* chosen community, overriding all distinctions of neighborhood, class lines, nationality, or culture. A man did not think of himself primarily as a member of this or that particular local church, as do so many American Protestants, but as a member of Christ's one body.

This consciousness of the community of all Christians everywhere was nourished especially by two dramatic ceremonies Jesus had commended to his disciples as symbols of the life of the Kingdom before there was any thought of a "church." Many of Jesus' disciples probably came to him from John the Baptist. In any case the followers of Jesus adopted John's practice of a ceremonial bath as a sign of the washing away of sins in repentance. In addition to this rite of initiation into the new "body," the disciples preserved at their regular

meal together the dramatized parable Jesus had presented
to the twelve on the night in which he was betrayed. In the
joy of the vindication of the resurrection they remembered
the obedience unto death which had sealed the new covenant
and rejoiced in the experience of Christ's continued fellowship. To this very day in the evangelical Lord's Supper the
experience of the disciples at Emmaus is repeated again and
again. Men have departed from the table-fellowship of
Christians with a sudden recognition that the living Christ
had been present among them, and have said to each other
in wondering joy, "Did not our hearts glow within us?"
The consecration of the brotherhood to the mind of Christ,
as his new body, was symbolized here, and also the mutuality
within the group. The gospel was preached thus in symbol
before it was written in Scripture and before any church
organization was established. The church was first of all
a "communion of saints," a participation of each in the other
and of all in the life of God's Reign.

The continued postponement of the full triumph of the
Kingdom, however, led the fellowship to adopt institutional
means to preserve its mission and message. The passing
away of the personal friends of Jesus made the recording
of memoirs about him essential, and various collections of
deeds and sayings were compiled in diverse places. The
earliest of our present gospels, that of Mark, was composed
at the end of this first generation, very possibly incorporating
earlier documents. Luke, still later, described how he had
gathered the accounts of several writers together, and that
Matthew did the same is evident from his incorporation of
nearly all of the text of Mark. Other gospels were also
compiled, some of which we know in scraps and fragments,
and various churches in various parts of the Mediterranean
world treasured one or another of these accounts. The latest
gospel was that of John, written about the beginning of the
second century.

In addition to a common ritual and a growing literary tradition, the Christian community gradually developed an organization. The early churches lived like those on the American frontier. There were no trained and established clergy; little companies were gathered here and there by circuit-riding evangelists, Paul, Prisca, Aquila, Apollos. What organization they had was usually on the synagogue pattern where an executive committee or sanhedrin of elders, also called "bishops" and "presbyters," carried on the necessary administrative responsibility. It was the traveling evangelists and prophets who were the spiritual authorities. Some of them, however, evidently abused the confidence placed in them, and the churches began to feel an increasing need for a criterion for testing spiritual claims. The local elders gained weight as stabilizing influences in proportion as the claims of missionary evangelists came under closer scrutiny. The pattern of local government, however, was not everywhere the same. Some churches, like Corinth and Rome, evidently were directed by a board of elders into the second century, while at Antioch responsibility was concentrated early in the single pastor. The superior efficiency of the latter procedure was doubtless the chief factor in its widespread adoption in the second century. There are thus historical precedents in the early church for the Congregational and Baptist type of church organization as well as the Presbyterian. And while diocesan bishops of the modern Episcopal and Roman Catholic type were not developed for many generations, nevertheless the high-church claim for the divine authority of the clergy over the laity finds a very early expression in Ignatius of Antioch. Historical scholarship recognizes a limited validity to all of these claims and by that fact denies the possibility of any one validly to assert exclusive divine sanction for itself. The debates over the proper organization of the churches must be settled on other grounds.

Questions of belief likewise were in the hands of the local congregations. From the beginning the ceremony of baptism had been accompanied by a profession of faith. The simplest must have been some variation of "I believe Jesus to be the Messiah." Our so-called "Apostles' Creed" developed from a baptismal confession used at the church in Rome. This freedom for local variation, much as exercised by the creeds of individual Baptist congregations in America today, led to divergencies of interpretation. Some insisted, for example, that Christians must submit to Jewish food laws and circumcision. Among the new converts of Hellenistic background, on the other hand, there was a tendency to develop Christianity into elaborate mythological and theosophical speculations. These "gnostics," as they were called, were in danger of losing all sense of historical reality in fantastic symbolism, and in their denial of the body and this world as beyond hope of redemption they never grasped the Christian victory over sin and death. Christian Science (gnosis means science) is a form of modern gnosticism which denies the reality of evil and death and consequently the actuality of Jesus' passion and resurrection. Like Mary Baker Eddy, the ancient Christian "Scientists" also produced their reinterpretations of the gospel history.

To counteract these anarchical dangers the church institution was still further developed in the course of the second century. Many of these discordant groups were making the claim, repeatedly used down the centuries and not least by Rome, that their peculiar conceptions were founded on unwritten teachings of Jesus, whether preserved by oral tradition or communicated in visions. The variegated literature as to the nature of Jesus' gospel required sifting so that an agreement could be secured as to which books and interpretations were to be approved for public worship. The first fruits of this process of "higher criticism" was a consensus on four of the many gospels in circulation as being the most reliable, together with the letters of the apostle Paul. The nucleus of a "new testament" to set beside the Jewish testament was established. All private revelations and traditions must henceforth be measured by this common and objective standard, the historical record of God's revelation in Jesus Christ. The second century church was thus forced to the Protestant insight that the only criterion of conflicting traditions or illuminations by the Inner Light is history, the Bible, the earliest and best records of God's work in Christ. This does not mean that the Bible is necessarily the primary means by which men are first brought to the gospel. On the contrary, the Reformers emphasized that men first find the gospel in the living tradition of the church, in the lives of believing parents or friends. And only so are men brought to understand the Bible, through the living fellowship and in it. And yet time and again that living tradition must be judged and reformed by the final authority in Christianity, the gospel.

The church universal and "catholic" as it emerged from these struggles after the middle of the second century was a federation of congregations, united in creed and scripture and in the government of a settled clergy. Thus the word "catholic" had shifted its meaning from an expression of the religious consciousness of the unity of Christ's body everywhere to refer to a concrete institutional federation. The dominant meaning was no longer "universal" but "orthodox." Congregations without the regular ministry, or with other sacred books or creeds, and there were multitudes of them, perhaps even a majority of would-be Christians, were now outside the "catholic" church.

Such an institutionalizing of the Christian fellowship was the first illustration of a pattern which has repeated itself dozens of times in every branch of the later history of Christianity. Every creative awakening of Christian life has passed after about two generations into a period of lowered inspiration, of organization and codification. This happened with each of the great monastic revivals of the middle ages, with the Continental Reformation, with English and American Puritanism in the seventeenth century, with Methodism and the American Great Awakening in the eighteenth. In all these cases, and many others, a period akin to the age of the apostles was swiftly followed by a generation or two of the temper characteristic of the first half of the second century. The writers of the second century show no comprehension of Paul's intense awareness of the presence and redeeming power of God. Instead of accepting the forgiveness offered in Christ in trust, they set about *earning* their salvation in precisely the Pharisaic style Paul and Jesus had transcended. Tertullian, for example, discusses the penitential acts of a Christian, not as the expression of a contrite heart in gratitude for a forgiveness it could never earn, but as actual compensations and merits before God. Personal religious awareness of God's action faded away and men concentrated more on human responsibility for leading a good life. In the face of Jesus' advice that the best of saints should know themselves "unprofitable· servants" and never presume to count their virtues as merits before God like the Pharisee, it was now blandly assumed that men could be good "over and above the commandment of God," and that, on the other hand, the giving of alms to the poor could buy the forgiveness of God for sins. Religion had ceased to be the life of faith in God and became a man-centered cultivation of morality. We, too, are living at the end of a period of moralism and man-centered religion.

A second type of false security before God which tends to arise in these less heroic ages is a reliance on the religious institution in place of God. Down through the centuries Christians have again and again stood in need of the warning John addressed to the Jews, "Say not to yourselves 'We are sons of Abraham'," and the similar point Paul urged with regard to circumcision. It is widely supposed that membership in the Jesuit order ensures salvation, just as in the middle ages a similar superstition about the Franciscans led to strange death-bed scenes in which dying reprobates were clothed with the Franciscan garb. The construction of an "orthodox" institution in the second century opened the way to this kind of evasion of personal repentance and submission to God. No doubt there will be Protestants at the Last Judgment whose only defense will be that they were always faithful churchmen and believed what they were told.

An institutional and external conception of the succession from the apostles, moreover, was developing in this period. There was grave need, as we have seen, for some criterion of evangelical faith and practice amid the controversies, and those churches, like Jerusalem, Antioch, Rome, and Alexandria, whose local traditions went back to the earliest days, were looked to for guidance. The opinions of those apostolic foundations carried such weight that it became very important to demonstrate the antiquity and continuity of their traditions. Much as newly rich families suddenly acquire descent from Richard the Lion-Hearted or William the Conqueror, so lists of the succession of bishops in Rome and elsewhere now appeared as credentials. Out of recollections of names of earlier elders, for example, the Roman church pieced together an unbroken line back to "bishop" Peter. The episcopal status, and even the existence of these "bishops," of course, was highly dubious for the period anterior to the memories of the living generation. The pastor of the Roman congregation, however, had other recommendations than the inherited mantles of both Peter and Paul. He presided over the largest and wealthiest congregation of the Christian world, and one made up, as was natural in the capital city, of members transferred from other congregations all over the empire. He was consequently called upon to arbitrate differences between congregations more often than the others. Men who supported this leadership of the bishop of Rome, like Irenaeus and Cyprian, however, never hesitated to call him to account when he, too, fell into error on interpretations of the faith, and Alexandria, Antioch, and Jerusalem, especially, defended jealously their equal claims to apostolic authority. In reaction against this whole tendency to solidify the church into a "battalion of bishops," as Tertullian expressed it, there arose major revolts. While these schismatic groups, like many such, went to fanatical extremes, they also embodied a genuine evangelical appeal to the priesthood of all believers and a warning to all regularly ordained clergy that the true apostolic succession lies not in external and official devolution from the apostles, but in being like them.

Constantine and Eastern Orthodoxy

Early in the fourth century occurred the most far-reaching change in the status and character of Christianity since the days of Paul. The pagan Emperor Constantine, whether from superstitious fear or from calculations of expediency, reversed the policy of persecution and sought to use Christianity as a cohesive bond in his disintegrating empire. For three centuries Christians had been segregated in the Empire as Negroes are in the modern United States. Periodically they had endured lynching, and, toward the end, state attempts at complete suppression. Their business, recreation, and personal relations had been to a remarkable degree confined to their own fellowship and their moral standards were conspicuously higher than those of the society about them. They had made no serious effort to master and transform the pagan civilization about them, but had lived apart, nonpolitical and predominantly pacifist, a suffering minority. But now with the Constantinian revolution this high visibility of the Christian fellowship became obscured, and, as has been the case with the church in Western civilization ever since in large measure, it became hard to tell Christian from non-Christian on a working-day. For the first time in its history the Christian church was swamped with what the Younger Churches of Asia know as "rice Christians," men and women seeking social or political advantages. Henceforth the question would rise periodically, "Is there any wheat among the tares?" And it would be the radical separatists of the Reformation who would first recapture the full earnestness of the martyr spirit and the holy remnant of the pre-Constantinian church.

Just as we might take the Anabaptist communities of South Dakota as perhaps the best living expression of the radical wing of the Reformation and also the pre-Constantinian church, so we would find the living tradition of the church of the fourth and fifth centuries best of all in Eastern Orthodoxy. The most powerful and important of the sections of Eastern Orthodoxy today is, of course, the Russian Orthodox Church. With it may be grouped, however, some twenty churches of a similar type, chiefly located in the Balkans and the Near East. All together they represent nearly a third of all Christians, and a third type of Christianity which is neither Protestant nor Roman Catholic, but antedates both in its unbroken continuity from the fourth and fifth centuries. Some understanding of Eastern Orthodoxy is thus important as providing another perspective on the character of evangelical Protestantism, as well as for pressing practical questions which arise from the relationship of Orthodox Catholics to evangelicals both in the World Council of Churches and in the Federal Council of Churches in the United States.

The only associations most American Protestants have ever had with Orthodox Catholicism have come from visits to the elaborate liturgical services at Easter, perhaps, in the curious onion-domed churches to be found in many industrial cities of the North. Indeed no other church, Protestant or Catholic, rivals the liturgical splendor and magnificence of

Orthodoxy, which is sacramental Christianity *par excellence*.
This splendor dates in large measure from the fourth and
fifth centuries when the worship of the early Christians was
swiftly elaborated to suit the new social position. The men
and women who gathered for Christian worship were no
longer knit by intimate bonds such as prompted the mutual
economic aid of the early church. The rich were now willing
to listen to fine preaching from an Ambrose or Chrysostom
and to contribute to great philanthropic undertakings, but
they had no intention of removing the barriers that hindered
full community with the poor. Civic and political interests
now claimed religious sanction and support where earlier
Christians had looked rather to the coming Kingdom. In
proportion as the common life of the Christian fellowship
was increasingly divided by class and cultural loyalties, so
the character of Christian worship changed. The sacraments
in the pre-Constantinian and Anabaptist conception are cele-
brations of the felt redemption of the common life, and, as
such, intensifications of it. Now, in the absence of any such
conscious community in the congregations, the sacraments
were less to celebrate, than to *create,* a sense of mystical
brotherhood. This called for a great elaboration of liturgy
and architectural magnificence and every conceivable acces-
sory to create a mood of participation in a mystical body so
conspicuously contrasted to social and ethical realities. The
Russian word *sobornost,* which means "cathedralness" and
"togetherness," is a clue to the nature of this sacramental life
in which men patricipate in the body of Christ although
nearly every aspect of their daily human relations would
seem to deny it. This association of the sacrament with the
common life, however attenuated, provides a common
ground for evangelicals and Orthodox which does not exist
between evangelicals and Romanists. Orthodoxy did not
degrade, materialize, and commercialize the sacraments,
either the Eucharist or penance, as did the Roman church in

the middle ages, with its indulgences, purchased private masses, and the magical abuses associated with transubstantiation, against which the Reformation rose in holy indignation.

In various other respects, similarly, Eastern Orthodoxy is closer to evangelical Protestantism than is Roman Catholicism. Both types of Catholicism teach that the true church is defined by the institutional clergy empowered to perform certain liturgical acts. There is reason to think, however, that in Orthodoxy the religious life was freer. The laity were encouraged to read the Bible, for example, and to form their devotional life upon it. They preserved a hope of a fulfillment of love and justice in a coming Kingdom and did not accept the Roman identification of the Kingdom with the rule of the clerical hierarchy. The people cultivated and honored spiritual stature more than ecclesiastical, and "saints" seem to have played a more independent and important role in contrast to prelates than in the Roman church. Finally, by its conception of the government of the church as vested in councils such as those of the fourth and fifth centuries, expressing the moral consensus of the whole, Orthodox Catholicism is nearer to evangelical Protestantism than either is to the spiritual despotism of the modern papal court over its purely passive subjects. Evangelicals and Orthodox Catholics can carry on a discussion. There is no discussion with Rome, only submission or rejection. "Paul is here, and John," it was said at one of the great conferences of the universal church in the 1920's, "but Peter is still absent."

With regard to the definition of the Christian gospel, however, evangelicals and Orthodox Catholics find themselves in some tension. It is the boast of Orthodoxy that it adheres to the doctrinal decisions of the early councils of the church, especially those of the fourth and fifth centuries, every jot and tittle, without any such amendments or modifications as have since been introduced both by Romanists and by Protestants. For Orthodoxy, consequently, the doctrine of Christianity has been stated finally and irrevocably in the language and philosophical concepts of the creeds of the fourth and fifth centuries, and it is neither to be added to nor reinterpreted in the terms of other cultural situations. The "Nicene" and "Athanasian" Creeds and the formula of Chalcedon state for all eternity what a Christian believes and how he conceives that belief. While a majority of evangelicals have probably always been willing to subscribe to these creeds, they have never accepted them as final or infallible. The creeds are authoritative for evangelicals, but only because and in so far as they adequately indicate the gospel message. And that Word of God must be freshly heard and interpreted in every situation. Orthodox Catholicism thus presents a static traditionalism in contrast to the dynamic evangelical conception of the church. Within the last century, however, Russian Orthodoxy has produced a school of thinkers, notably Soloviev, Dostoievsky and Berdiaev, who have left mere traditionalism and in some ways come very near the evangelical view.

Perhaps the most conspicuous present-day legacy from the Constantinian revolution is the tradition of subserviency to the state which Orthodox Catholicism has retained ever since. Today the problem is how far Russian Orthodoxy has become simply the tool of Kremlin policy. This cloven hoof of purely worldly policy was to be discerned as the chief active agent in the first formal definition of an orthodox creed. Constantine had adopted the church as a political instrument of unification. When he discovered to his annoyance that there was theological dissension within the church, he summoned the clergy to a conference and urged them to come to an agreement as soon as possible. He enforced this recommendation by punishing the minority who opposed the decisions of the council. And from this beginning was to grow the use of the police power to coerce heretics, a practice which has since been used in varying degree by all three branches of the faith, Orthodox, Roman Catholic, and Protestant. It must be admitted that this subserviency of Orthodoxy to the state, a system sometimes described as "Caesaropapism," has found Protestant imitators in certain Lutheran and Anglican groups. American Protestantism, by contrast, overwhelmingly Puritan in tradition, is as alien to this conception of the church's role as is Roman Catholicism. Where this system is defended on higher grounds than mere flattery of power, it usually derives from a very idealistic and otherworldly notion of the church which is careless of mundane affairs and abandons any prophetic office. Such seems to be the case with Russian Orthodoxy today, a circumstance no doubt heightened by the appalling persecution to which it was subjected in the twenties and thirties by the Soviets.

Caesaro-papism was especially ruinous in the fourth and fifth centuries because the state was disintegrating. With orthodoxy defined as the church of the emperor, the revolt of the major provinces became theological as well as political. A large commixture of political and cultural nationalism with religion shattered "Christendom," much as was to happen again in the fifteenth and sixteenth centuries in Europe. The major Asian and African provinces of the crumbling Roman Empire adopted one "heresy" or another, largely for political reasons. Many of these separated Eastern churches still exist as small communities, the Copts of Egypt and Abyssinia, the Nestorians and Jacobites of Asia Minor and Syria. Had they not borne the brunt of the Moslem invasion they might today constitute churches as large as the Roman Catholic or the Protestant, and their theological peculiarities would be exercising the scholars of the ecumenical movement. Had they not suffered so terribly they would also have made it impossible for Christianity ever to seem to be a religion based on Europe, or a religion of the white races, for it was neither in the fourth and fifth centuries.

Chapter II

The Western Church in the Middle Ages

∩∩∩

The Evangelical Undertow

IN REBELLION against the vast secularization of the church after Constantine, and in despair of civilized life in the manifest collapse of world organization, there arose a great evangelical revival of the laity to assert the demands of the Kingdom in actual fellowship as well as in mere sacramental communion. For a millennium to come the heroic witness to the gospel was to find expression in a series of monastic revivals, culminating in the Reformation. These were the evangelical Puritans and Calvinists of the "middle ages," insisting on the dedication of the whole common life to Christian obedience, and on the full religious and moral responsibility of the laymen, even in ministering to each other. Basil of Caesarea, John Cassian, Cassiodorus, and Benedict established the pattern of Christian communities which soon dotted Europe as cultural and economic as well as religious seedbeds. Time and again the religious impulse failed and monasticism lapsed into worldliness, wealth, sexual immorality. When has any great religious awakening outlasted two or three generations? But then would come a reform tide out of Cluny, or Citeaux, or with a Francis of Assisi. We should not let the Reformation attack on monastic faults blind us to the fact that the attack was itself fundamentally one of these reforming crusades of the monastic spirit. Much of the pre-history of Protestantism is, for the medieval period, the history of monastic revivals.

The evangelical vitality of monasticism was successfully related to the sacramental institutional church by the formula of a double standard in Christianity. The monks took seriously the Kingdom requirement of perfection, but the ordinary layman was assured that he could still know Christian redemption by participation in the sacramental life of the church provided only he manifested certain minimum evidences of respectability. Some such theory as this seemed inevitable in a day when the church was full of people who had only the crudest notion of the meaning of the Christian gospel. Most of our barbarian ancestors were converted to Christianity in the early middle ages by tribes or villages, as has been happening recently in India. Those who enter the faith in wholesale lots will not be expected to prove model Christians at once. The time would come, however, when it would seem plausible that religious Europe had outgrown her minority and could be universally challenged by the whole gospel, with no double standards.

For generations, meanwhile, the laity were too used to isolation and submission before the external authority to understand the corporate character of true Christian community, and to rise to its assertion. The monastics and friars knew the meaning of community and evangelical faith, but the hierarchy was content to leave the full gospel to them, keeping the laity in general in a kind of permanent minority status in religion, on the principle of a double ethic and "implicit" faith. The level of lay religion, however, was rising steadily through these centuries toward the Reformation. The earlier great development of superstition, images, relics, saint-worship, Mariolatry had come with the lowering of the cultural level of the church and popular incapacity to read the Bible. But with the rise of the towns in the twelfth and thirteenth centuries came a revival of education and the beginnings of a new literate and disciplined laity capable of discriminating between such semi-paganism and a more mature religion.

The new life appeared first in Italy, of course, and in a sense the Franciscan movement *was* the Italian Reformation. From Peter Waldo, Francis' predecessor in evangelical simplicity, stem the Waldensians, the oldest Protestant church. The great Franciscan preachers antedated the Reformers in their estimate of the relative significance of the preaching of the Word and the attendance at badly-understood sacraments. The response of whole communities, men, women, and children, and the desire of all to become friars likewise antedated the Reformation rejection of the double standard in religion. Laymen discovered the Bible was not beyond their capacities, as the priests were wont to tell them, and Waldensians in Italy and France, Lollards in England, Hussites in Bohemia, showed a readiness and ability to grasp the gospel in their native languages without hierarchical glosses. The increased use of catechisms and devotional reading and of the vernacular in services marked this fresh response.

The rising tide of lay religion was also a group movement, a recovery of the corporate nature of the Christian life. In worship the recovered sense of the church as a religious fellowship rather than a mechanical dispensary of *mana* began to make its way. Wiclif and Huss drew on Augustine's view of the true church as the people gathered by God, in contrast to the institution drained of mutuality. Eck was later to persuade Luther that he had been a Hussite without knowing it. Part of the Hussite demand was for increased lay participation in the sacraments, in particular the use of the language understood by the congregation and the right of the laity to obey the injunction "Drink ye, *all*, of it," a right denied by the priests out of superstitious fear lest the blood of Christ be spilled. This participation of the community in the sacraments was to increase to the great sacramental revival of the Reformation in which Luther and Calvin were to urge the weekly observance of the Lord's Supper by all after the manner of the early church.

The idea of dedicated living likewise began to creep over monastery walls to lay brotherhoods and "third orders" and various semi-monastic communities like the Brethren of the Common Life, the Friends of God. In these revivals of Christian fellowship, which produced devotional classics like the *Imitation of Christ* and the *Theologia Germanica*, there was a recovery of personal communion with God which imperceptibly displaced the ecclesiastical sacramental machinery from its monopoly to the position of a not indispensable auxiliary. And with the recovery of the community came the fresh understanding of the element of promise in the preaching of the Kingdom. For almost a thousand years Augustine's identification of the Reign of Christ with the government of the clergy had stood, but from the days of Joachim of Fiore the ancient hope of a growing fulfillment, a coming "age of the spirit," stirred men again to a sense of the living God in their historical present and imminent future.

In all these ways local religious groups were discovering again the true nature of the church for generations before the Reformation gave a clear definition of it. In medieval theory the marks of the true visible church were reduced to the clerical closed shop union and its ceremonies. Apart from that, it was taught, God's work of reconciling the world in Christ does not normally go on. But thousands and thousands of Christians had come to personal communion with God more or less independently of the mechanical sacraments and were prepared for the Reformation recognition of the true church as visible wherever an active trusting response to God's invitation in Christ manifests itself in the life of a fellowship.

Papalism

But while the monks and lay brothers of some thirty
generations were thus nourishing in holes and corners the
spirit of the evangelical fellowship, the specifically Roman
Catholic system of church government and church and state
relations was being worked out. Just as Orthodoxy seeks to
preserve intact the fourth and fifth century church, so modern
Romanism, despite extensive modifications in the Counter-
Reformation, still yearns back to *its* "age of faith," the thirteenth century. If we would understand Roman Catholicism
and Protestantism then, we must look at the high middle
ages as well as at the sixteenth century. Three striking new
developments in the church require mention, first, the claim
of the bishop of Rome to ecclesiastical and religious authority
over all Christians, second, the claim of that bishop to political authority over all governments, and, third, the claim
of the papal hierarchy to control all aspects of social life,
economic, legal, intellectual. By surveying each of these
aspects of medieval Catholicism briefly we may gain greater
clarity on the corresponding aspects of Protestantism.

While the thirteenth century is the apex of medieval
Roman Catholicism, the Roman "Reformation" began in the
middle eleventh century in the generation that saw the Nor-
man conquest of England. The invention of the papacy as
a world power in that generation was the work to an amazing
degree of one man, the Roman Catholic Calvin, one of the
molders of world history whom even Napoleon envied,
Hildebrand. Hildebrand's program was to make the papal
church an independent and universal religious and political
power.

Let us begin with the question of papal authority over
all Christians. The first startling evidence of a new and
aggressive determination at this point came with the final
and decisive "excommunication" of the Orthodox Catholics

in 1054. It will be recalled that the Ancient Church had
conceded to the bishop of Rome a primacy of honor, but
no special authority or jurisdiction outside his own diocese.
In the great councils of the fourth and fifth centuries which
determined the issues of faith and morals for all Christians,
the bishop of Rome participated with other bishops equally,
and often contributed less than his share.

The barbarian invasions, however, changed the situation.
Like the other provinces of the Roman Empire, the Latin-
speaking West and its churches were cut off from the emperor and the imperial church at Constantinople. Education
collapsed and with it the cultural level generally and the
understanding and awareness in the West of the greater
church became increasingly difficult. Under these circumstances certain new claims of the bishops of Rome to rights
of jurisdiction over all Christians gradually established themselves in Western opinion. The more cultured and ecclesiastically impressive East was little disturbed, on the other
hand, by the pretensions of these bishops of the barbarians
who had lost even the language of the ancient church. The
papal claims were simply denied as often as they were
presented.

What was the basis of these claims? It will be worth the
time to notice them, because Roman Catholicism makes the
same plea still. Some ingenious lawyer apparently invented
the argument in the third or fourth century. It all rested on
a new interpretation of that passage in Matthew (16: 18, 19)
which follows Peter's first profession of conviction that Jesus
was the Messiah. The words of Jesus in reply are "Now I
tell you, Peter is your name, and on this rock (Greek
"petra") I will build my church. . . . Whatever you prohibit
on earth will be prohibited in heaven, and whatever you permit on earth will be permitted in heaven." The majority of
of fathers, ancient and medieval, agreed that the cornerstone
referred to in this passage meant the conviction that Jesus

was the Messiah, and that to the whole fellowship sharing
that conviction was given the authority of the "power of the
keys." The new interpretation, however, urged that it was
Peter himself who was made cornerstone and authority for
the church, and that when he died this authority was trans-
mitted to the bishops of Rome in succession.* In the ignorance and isolation of the Latin church of the time of the

---

* We may make three comments. First of all, there is the virtual certainty that this passage is apocryphal, and that Jesus never said these
words at all. As we have seen, he preached a Kingdom at hand and had
no thought of a continuing "church." This is the only time, in fact, that
the word "church" is put in his mouth, and the two earlier gospels which
tell the story of Peter's profession of faith do not mention the "church."
This late and isolated passage cannot be reconciled to the great body
and main trend of Jesus' teaching of the Kingdom.

In the second place, the interpretation placed on the passage by the
majority of the fathers is clearly more in accord with the rest of Jesus'
teaching and the witness of Paul than is the Roman view. Jesus had
made it clear that preeminence in the Kingdom was not to be after the
fashion of princes, even princes of the church, but the wholly non-
authoritarian leadership of the saintly and humble. It is very strange,
moreover, if Jesus had assigned authority to Peter, that he should turn
upon him immediately, as he does, with the fierce rebuke "Get behind
me, you Satan! . . . Your outlook is not God's but man's." It is very
strange, if Jesus was known to have assigned authority to Peter, that the
recognized head of the Jerusalem fellowship was Jesus' brother James,
and that Paul criticized Peter as a weak and unreliable disciple with no
special prerogatives.

But even assuming this dubious grant of authority to Peter, in the
third place, there is no authority whatever for its transfer to the bishops
of Rome. Of course, Peter may have gone to Rome and become head of
the Christian community there. So may have all the rest of the twelve.
All we need is evidence. And supposing that Peter had these powers he
apparently never exerted, and supposing he went to Rome, which is not
unlikely, by what right did he transmit these prerogatives to the bishops
of Rome? And how could he do so, if there were no bishops of Rome
before the second century?

Despite these difficulties and others, the whole case for the authority
of the Roman popes in the church rests on this solitary passage. For its
sake Rome insists that Matthew was the earliest gospel, winking at the
obvious fact that Matthew has copied over five-sixths of Mark, often word
for word.

invasions such an interpretation seemed plausible and gradually established itself as the natural meaning of the passage.

The eleventh century, as we have seen, witnessed a new determination to enforce the implications of this deed of jurisdiction from Jesus Christ. At long last, in pursuance of the threat of Leo IX to "scrub its mangey hide with vinegar and salt," the papacy finally and solemnly broke communion with the Eastern church. The latter responded in kind.

Hildebrand had more difficult problems than this to face at home. The Latin church was in danger of becoming completely assimilated to the feudal political structure, much as in our own day the church is in danger of being assimilated to the several national states. The great problem was to get churchmen independent of local political control and to make possible an effective universal organization. It was primarily for this reason that Hildebrand decided Catholic priests should not have wives and families, which would be hostages to political rulers. An even more bitter resistance met the pope's attempt to secure from rulers the patronage of ecclesiastical offices, especially bishops. Similarly, precautions were taken to guard the elections of popes themselves from interference from outside the church officials. In all this Hildebrand was only partially successful, but his successors persisted, and built an independent and self-governing ecclesiastical structure over all Europe.

But this was only half of the program. The ecclesiastical machine was not merely to be independent of local rulers in religious matters; it was to be supreme over them in political affairs. By what right? As with the case of ecclesiastical jurisdiction, many generations had established and sanctified what was legally a more than dubious claim. Half a millennium earlier, the invading barbarians had found that the bishops of Rome were the only public authorities left in Italy who had resources of money and ships, and with whom

they could negotiate. Out of simple necessity the popes had
become heirs of the emperor's political authority in Italy.
Within a few centuries some obliging forgers were buttress-
ing this *de facto* political power by documents purporting to
record an assignment by Constantine to the popes of political
jurisdiction in the West. These forgeries were incorporated
into church law by the high middle ages and quite deceived
such thinkers as Thomas Aquinas. They were exposed at
the Reformation but almost to a man the bishops of the
Counter-reformation council of Trent believed in them and
built the political ambitions of modern Roman Catholicism
on them.

While not all Catholics by any means drew from this
claim the program of making the papacy the divine-right
monarchy of all Europe, nevertheless, in many ways the
papal church was the only real "state" in the middle ages. It
was the popes who first gained the credit of turning quar-
reling barons to the Crusades and thus awakening a sense
of European community as against Islam. Out of the contributions for the crusade the papacy created the first tax system of Europe. In a day when half the land of France and
Germany belonged to the church, the income of the pope
was far greater than that of any other crowned head. Innocent III coerced the kings of both England and France to
obedience by the use of the interdict, and actually appointed
rulers for the Empire. Such "supremacy" over political
rulers was, to be sure, short-lived, but the continued Roman
ambition for it has raised political problems into our own
day, and constitutes a fundamental contrast with Protestant
conceptions of church-state relations.

The third aspect of medieval Roman Catholicism which
we should notice was its revolutionary attempt to construct
a Christian civilization. The early church, it will be recalled,
existed for some three hundred years as a kind of foreign
body encysted within Greek and Roman pagan civilization.

Even after the adoption of Christianity by the dying Empire the age-old patterns of non-Christian culture defied any profound influence of Christianity. This same relationship continued between the Greek-speaking church and the Byzantine Empire in the Middle Ages, with the church never able to be much more than the department of religion in the government, so far as social impact was concerned. When Orthodoxy was carried north into the barbarian Slavic lands, as Latin Christianity was carried to the Teutonic barbarians, it would seem to have been too far emasculated ethically by its long subservience to seize the opportunity of constructing a "Christian civilization." That was the achievement, for the first time in Christian history, of the Latin church of the high Middle Ages. Political, economic, and cultural life were all related in some way to Christian loyalties. The relation was often of the most superficial sort, to be sure, but no such possibility had ever been realized before. This medieval attempt consisted chiefly in the arbitration or regulation of social decisions by the priestly caste. Generations were thus educated to submit their economic, political, legal, and intellectual activities to a more or less Christian ethical standard. Then the Puritan wing of Protestantism would be able to extend and deepen this Christian penetration of civilization, regulating "worldly" activities now from within by the responsible and dedicated Christian conscience, instead of from without by the hierarchy. The scope and audacity of the medieval effort claim Protestant homage as the first mighty expression of what is now often taken to be the peculiarly American Protestant ambition to mold all social and political life to the pattern of the Kingdom of God.

The medieval papacy paid a high price for its ambitions, however, especially its claim for political supremacy. In the desperate struggle to maintain or recover its political dominance of Europe, the papal monarchy utilized and sacrificed its religious authority and irreparably damaged its spiritual

stature in the judgment of Christendom. Innocent III is
reported to have told Francis of Assisi at their first meeting
to go back to the pigsty, and one may well doubt whether
he was moved to such advice only by the smell of the un-
washed poor. The evangelical community in the role of
Suffering Servant was a standing reproach to the papal kingdom of the world. In the next century a pope who hunted
the radical Franciscans to the death was spending two-thirds
of the income that came to the Holy See on his *military*
budget. While the story of Constantine's donation of authority to the Bishop of Rome is a fraud, it symbolizes a profound truth in this connection. Before many centuries had
passed, Roman bishops performed precisely the role in the
councils of the church which the pagan Emperor had played
before them. While the early Christians died rather than
bow down to Caesar and the service of political power and
expediency, medieval and modern Roman Catholics were
to sacrifice more than incense to Caesarism. The papacy, as
Hobbes remarked, appears as the ghost of the Roman Empire
sitting crowned upon its grave. And for reasons Constantine
would understand the new papal Caesardom has shed, as the
historian Lecky estimated, more innocent blood than any
other institution in human history. She has never expressed
remorse nor denied her right to persecute again, nor does she
stay her hand where she has the power today, as in Spain or
Peru. The Reformation does not show a clean slate in this
regard, either, but Protestant persecution in total was half-
hearted and trifling compared to the butchery of the Inquisition. And Protestantism has repented.

It was the attempt to assert political supremacy, also, which
reduced the papacy to such a low reputation that medieval
Catholicism actually returned momentarily to the representative government of the early church. For two generations
the papacy had been separated from Rome and established
on the French border. Peoples unfriendly to France conse-

quently distrusted papal policy, just as in our own day democratic nations have thought they discerned a dangerous convergence of the policy of the Vatican with fascism in all
the Latin countries. And no sooner was the papacy freed
from this "captivity" to France, than the cardinals themselves scandalized Christendom by producing *two* rival
popes. From this outrageous situation the earnest Christians
of the Latin West now turned back from Hildebrand to the
constitution of the early church. The reforms needed
throughout the life of the church might, it was hoped, be
secured by the representative organization of the church in
council. Though discredited, the papal absolutism consistently evaded such reform for excellent financial reasons.

The "conciliarist" movement was first given its program
early in the fourteenth century by Marsilius of Padua. Paris,
the greatest university of Europe, thereafter provided the
most consistent leadership. The choicest Christian thinkers
and churchmen of two centuries then pioneered on this
fundamental issue of the Reformation and in so doing were
direct predecessors of Luther, Calvin, Bullinger, Cranmer,
Melancthon, Knox. A series of councils of the whole Latin
church met a century before the Reformation. The Council
of Constance laid down the principle that the council represented the whole church and as such held its authority directly from Christ and was superior to the popes. At the
Councils of Basel and Ferrara-Florence a share in decisions
was extended, as in the early church, to parish clergy, and
laymen, chiefly members of university faculties and princes.
The former assembly redefined the papacy as the administrative head of the constitutional government of the church.
Unlike the Greek church, most of the spokesmen for councils believed that the church in council through its regular
representatives was authoritative but not infallible, since
there was no means of assuring that it adequately represented the true church. The only infallibility lay in the

revelation of the Scriptures, all organs of interpretation being fallible. The surest interpretation would come from the widest representation of the mind of the whole church, always open to correction and revision. The logic of this whole position is so familiar to an American audience as scarcely to need statement. Our theory of the achievement of justice by representative democracy is precisely the application to secular government of the conciliarist theory of the church brought to us through Protestantism. But while the Council of Constance demonstrated its superiority to the popes in fact as well as theory by a final healing of the schism, Martin V promptly broke his word and repudiated his obligations to the representatives of the church, restoring absolute rule. By their successful effort to stifle the witness of the Holy Spirit in the Christian community and by their support of intolerable moral and religious abuses, the popes of the fifteenth century thus made a revolt of evangelical catholics inevitable. And the heritage of representative and responsible government in the church was yielded by the default of the popes to Protestantism.

No Reform without Revolution

With the defeat of the conciliarist movement, the papacy confirmed in the church all sorts of corruption of the type found nowadays in such organizations as those of Pendergast or Hague. The rising tide of piety in the fifteenth century occurred outside the clergy and the centers of church government, where morality and spirituality were becoming ever more unusual. Ecclesiastical appointments at this time *normally* involved what our municipal bosses now call a shakedown. Men who would not receive promotion in the church by such means remained simple priests if they became clerics at all. A responsible abbot charged that priests were generally ignorant, addicted to drinking and gambling and more concerned to beget children than buy books. At the Council of Basel the Bishop of Lübeck soberly urged that priests be permitted to marry since "not one priest in a thousand" kept his vow of celibacy. With the clergy and curia developing unchecked in this direction under the Renaissance papacy, and the laity experiencing a widespread revival of religion, a rupture was inevitable.

When the Reformation came in that wonderful generation in the second quarter of the sixteenth century it burst forth almost simultaneously over most of Latin Christendom from the suppressed aspirations of centuries. Its leaders were all trained as Catholics and most of them had been ordained Catholic priests. Its most effective propagandists were simple clergy all over Europe who now found courage to say what had long lain on their consciences. Most of them had no intention of leaving the church of their fathers; they wished to reform it. These were no wanton revolutionaries. Luther himself had remained a submissive churchman and exemplary monk, vicar of eight monasteries, for ten years after he had discovered the meaning of evangelical reconciliation with God. He only discovered and defended the original conciliarist organization of the church after he had been shocked to find that the papal monarchy stood pat on outrageous corruption and thus raised in his mind the problem of its credentials.

The financial shenanigans which occasioned Luther's protest are more fully known to us than they were to him. The wealthy boy prince, Albert of Magdeburg, who was not old enough to be a bishop, had succeeded in having himself appointed to two bishoprics, and was enjoying their revenues. So satisfying did he find his career in the church that he offered to grease the palm of Leo X to gain yet a third bishopric. Leo, the Medici banker, who had announced the intention, when he accepted office, of "enjoying the papacy," suggested to Albert the appropriateness of a gift of twelve

thousand ducats "for the twelve apostles." Albert replied
with greater accuracy that he was only paying "for the seven
deadly sins." They settled on ten thousand. To help raise
funds for the bribe, Leo put at Albert's disposal the church's
staff of indulgence salesmen, whose sales talks, even in our
own day, seem so often to oversimplify the theological statement of just what the purchase of an indulgence accom-
plishes.

Luther, as a parish pastor, found that his people were
being told that they could buy for cash immunity from the
due consequences of sin. As the Catholic princes wrote
the pope five years after Luther posted his theses, "License
to sin with impunity is granted for money. . . . Hence come
fornications, adulteries, incests, perjuries, homicides, thefts,
and a whole hydra of evil." Luther had questioned the
whole assumption that men could profit by the ministry of
the saints, not by accepting the fellowship of their crosses,
but simply by a cash payment at the grilled window of the
Treasury of Merits on the Tiber. He denied that the papal
court had ever possessed the power to release men from
punishment, and asked the embarrassing question, supposing
that the pope has such power, "Why doesn't he empty
purgatory for the sake of the most holy charity" rather than
doing it only partially and only for money?

Only gradually did Luther perceive how this blasphemous
conception that priests were able to manipulate the Almighty
by incantations, formulas, and liturgical transactions had
pervaded the whole sacramental system of the church. Private masses, for example, were widely performed on the
assurance that God could so be put under obligation to perform whatever services the purchaser of the masses had in
mind. This was ordinary pagan conjuring and magic. Was
this the living God who could be summoned into a wafer
like a djinn from the *Arabian Nights* and then sent on
errands, or constrained to moderate his judgments of sinners

by the assurance of a priest that certain financial adjustments
had been made? Was there really any man on earth with
the power, in order to put pressure on wayward rulers, to
enjoin God from his eternal purpose of reconciliation in
their territories? But when Luther and the Catholic princes
addressed remonstrances to the papal court they looked to the
wrong quarters. That court set up a Commission of Cardinals to study the problem of reform, but when the prelates
submitted their report in 1537, it contained among many
damaging revelations the significant observation that the
source of all this corruption was the absolute dominion of
the Pope. The report was suppressed and the Roman
Gestapo, the Inquisition, was revived. Truly the Reformation had not come too soon. It was time that those who
believed in the Reign of God in Christ should reexamine the
Roman title to authority in the church.

That time is not yet over. "The moral salvation of the
papacy," said Jacob Burckhardt, "was due to its mortal enemies." The Reformation alone could force a house-cleaning,
and to this day the Roman church has never been able to
keep itself free from spiritual and moral rottenness except
in the presence of criticism from without. Consolidated into
a new sect at the Council of Trent, on principles we must
presently examine, Romanism has remained a caricature
of the gospel in the lands of the Mediterranean and Latin
America where it has been freed of criticism by Inquisition
and censorship. Roman Catholics admit that their communion is at its best in Protestant countries, Germany, England, Holland, the United States, or where, as in France, the
majority of the nation have declared their emancipation.
For the sake of vigorous and spiritual Romanism, the Protestant church remains today as necessary as at the Reformation. Modern Romanism cannot live of its own resources.
The road of spiritual despotism leads eternally to corruption
save when confronted by the force of moral example from

without. Thus the evangelical witness of Protestantism has made it possible for millions of evangelical Christians to live and die with only passing discomfort within the Roman church without becoming Protestants themselves. A Romanism which has repudiated the ancient conciliarist principle is ever afterward dependent for its religious integrity on a sister Protestantism.

Protestants who search their own history, however, will recognize the pains of readjustment and the temptations to which Romanism has succumbed only more completely than Protestantism. Protestants, also, as we are to show in the following chapters, have again and again yielded to the temptation to set up false securities, to seek salvation in institutional loyalties, moralism, creedal orthodoxies, or Biblical literalism, all substitutes for the personal trust in the living God and the acceptance of his free grace taught by the evangel. Not seldom in the course of its history, moreover, has Protestantism had occasion to be grateful for the Roman church. At the least, God has granted us hundreds and thousands of true lovers of Christ in the Roman communion who have been his ministers by their lives or writings to Protestants. The international organization of Romanism, again, has repeatedly been a reminder to Protestants that their loyalties ought not to be merely provincial. And by its very external rigidity Romanism, however indirectly, has served to remind many subjectivistic and humanistic Protestants of the objectivity and the superhuman authority of the Christian revelation. Perhaps the God who brings into existence that which does not exist, intends some new thing out of the complementary and mutually strengthening witnessing of the sister communions of the West.

Chapter III

Reformation and Counter-reformation

THE REFORMATION, like all revolutions, was a complicated and morally ambiguous movement. From the point of view of political history, the great significance of the sixteenth century is that it produced the modern national state. The pressures toward national concentrations of power had already broken the unity of Christendom before the Reformation. The papacy was already no longer able to coerce kings and had adopted a system of treaties with them called "concordats" which were a tacit admission of their actual independence. The religious conflict made evident and irreparable this fragmentation of medieval unity. Princes saw in the Reformation an opportunity to transfer to their own thrones some of the respect and loyalty hitherto yielded to the Roman popes. They also took advantage of the lowered prestige of the papacy to confiscate great wealth from it. The pressures toward this development are inextricably interwoven with the establishment of the chief Protestant churches in Germany, Holland, Scandinavia, England, Scotland, and, it may be observed, with the reorganization of Romanism in Spain, France, Italy, Austria. Similarly the maturing of the national cultures of the "Teutonic," non-Latin, peoples also played a role in their repudiation of the church of Latin culture. The shifts in social classes attendant on the great economic revolution likewise added secular motives for the support or rejection of the new religious movement. Other factors might be analyzed, but what must not be overlooked, as it sometimes is nowadays, is the great religious revival with its own energies and purposes, however much they were supported or perverted by secular forces. Let us first seek to understand the religious heart of the movement before try-ing to measure the degree of its subjugation to other interests.

Descriptions of the Reformation usually find their focus in the highly dramatic figure of Brother Martin Luther. Luther certainly set the match to the fuse. The power which drove him was just as certainly religious and the depths of this man's personal crises and insights make him one of the great sources for the student of prophetic faith and thought in all religious history. Luther's flair for colorful and exag-gerated language similarly suited him to become readily the object of popular hero worship. Thousands of children have thrilled over the story of Luther setting out to meet a very probable death at the sessions of Worms, determined to wit-ness to the truth though he meet "as many devils as tiles on the roof" and once there, ending his testimony with the (apocryphal) plea, "Here I stand. I can do no other. God help me. Amen." Controversialists have seized on Luther's intemperate expressions to quote him against himself, to prove him a violent authoritarian, an immoralist, a psycho-path. Millions have again been brought to peace with their God by means of his inspired German translation of the Bible. Every Christmas the world round hears his "Away in a manger, no crib for his bed." The thrilling Protestant battle-hymn, "A mighty fortress is our God," has given warn-ing to tyrants time after time, most recently in some of the crises of the second World War. And yet we must not permit this most impressive and dominating personality to interpret the whole Reformation for us. The various pressures and tendencies toward an evangelical church which we have been tracing would have eventuated in a Reforma-tion of some sort even without Luther. And Luther did not himself embody all these concerns; his peculiar emphases were to eventuate in only one of the continuing types of internal Protestant life. This is true even of his "justification by faith." We must make an effort to hold in mind at once the whole range of Protestant concerns and internal tensions, the three great conservative churches as well as the humanist and separatist liberal wing.*

Humanists, Separatists and Fellowships of the Spirit

We have declared that modern liberal Protestantism finds its chief affinity with the radical and partially suppressed wing of the Reformation. With them, consequently, our brief description of each of the main strands of Protestantism may well begin. The importance of the radical wing today does not lie in an institutional heritage. None of the six great families, Lutheran, Anglican, Presbyterian, Baptist, Methodist, or Congregationalist, traces back directly to the left-wing of the Reformation. The importance of the humanists and separatist "Anabaptists" for us today lies rather in the fact that their characteristic emphases have so largely established themselves within the formerly conservative churches.

We may begin with the Christian humanists, who represented the lay piety of the late middle ages among the intellectual aristocracy. Characteristic figures of this tendency were Ficino and Pico della Mirandola in Italy, Lefèvre d'Etaples in France, John Colet in England, and most famous of all, Erasmus. These were men who resented the scandalous moral abuses of the papal church, who detested the pedantic aridity of scholastic theology and were little concerned over institutional sacraments. They studied the Scriptures and the early writers of the church and wished for a return to the simple personal relation of man to God and the high morality of the early church. Within the Bible itself Erasmus turned back from Paul to what he took to be the

---

* cf. pages 17-18, above.

simpler religion and ethics of Jesus himself. In contrast to
the Lutheran and Calvinist notion of the ineradicable orneri-
ness of man, the humanists were relatively optimistic about
his moral possibilities. This included non-Christian man.
They were inclined to view Plato, Socrates, Cicero, and
Seneca as inspired as well as the Biblical prophets. They
thought in terms of a universal religion which found its
finest expression, no doubt, in the Bible, but was much more
comprehensive. The fatherhood of God and the brotherhood of man would suit the views of most of them. They
wanted reformation but deplored violence. Erasmus was
perhaps the first modern pacifist; he dreamed that men might
be reasonable and live together as brothers. It was no doubt
a superficial religion, but it had the non-too-common virtues
of common decency and common sense.

With views such as these the Christian humanists fell
pathetically between the warring systems of the sixteenth
century. Some tried to stay with Rome, but found themselves
increasingly under suspicion as dogmatisms hardened and
the Inquisition revived. Men like Erasmus, for whom there
was room in the broad and corrupt church of the Renaissance,
stood in danger of the stake in Tridentine Romanism. Nor
were Geneva or Wittenberg much more inviting. The most
congenial conception of the church for most humanists was
that of the little voluntary groups of those who separated
from *all* the great church-state systems. There were an indefinite variety of such little congregational churches which
sprang up especially in Switzerland and south Germany, and
many of them found their first leaders from the humanists.
The name of "re-baptizers," "Anabaptists," was generally
fastened on them because they usually considered the baptism
of children an empty ceremony. Baptism was only significant when the recipient really knew the baptism of the Spirit
in his personal experience and made a deliberate decision
for Christ. These little congregations were thus constituted

solely of convinced Christians, in contrast to the state churches which sought to include the whole community. They lived at a much higher pitch both of spiritual intensity and moral discipline, and as we noted earlier, recaptured for the first time the spirit of the early church before Constantine. They withdrew from "Christian" Europe and its great majority of immature or merely nominal Christians. They would usually refuse to hold political office, take judicial oaths, or engage in military service, all of which things they found expressly prohibited by Jesus. The great majority were gentle, peace-loving, dedicated Christians, claiming of state and society only the freedom to live as the gospel taught them and to preach that gospel to all the nations. It was they who taught Protestantism the missionary obligation.

Freedom, however, was universally denied them, and they were persecuted to the death by Romanists, Lutherans, and Calvinists alike. Under persecution they lost most of their educated leadership and became largely a movement of the lower classes. Persecution also encouraged fanaticism and radical manifestations in some quarters, such as communism and polygamy and a revived expectation of the imminent Second Coming of Christ. Thousands met cruel death with all the high devotion and courage of the early Christian martyrs. The largest single group of remnants was gathered up by Menno Simons, and in America to this day the Mennonites and Hutterites bear their witness against war. The parallel manifestations in the English-speaking world came with the Quakers of the seventeenth century, which was the century of the real religious reformation of the English people. It is the Quakers who have made us most aware, not only of the general Anabaptist desire for religious liberty and separation of church and state, but especially of their high ethical seriousness. Quaker contributions to the struggle against slavery, penal brutalities, and other social evils have changed the face of our society more than the efforts of other religious groups ten times their size. And surely the most authentic saint American Christianity has yet produced is John Woolman, the New Jersey Quaker.

Anglicans and Episcopalians

As we turn now from the persecuted undercurrents of the Reformation to the three great church systems which maintain their several traditions still, we are passing to churches which, like Rome, claimed the right to enforce their authority over all society. First of all, and most conservative of all, is the Anglican church, the parent of our Protestant Episcopal Church. Today the Anglicans and Episcopalians claim to have the only church which contains fully "Catholic" as well as fully Protestant wings. High Church Anglicans differ from Roman Catholics only in rejecting a few abuses of the medieval sacramental system and the authority of the pope. They feel themselves very close, consequently, to Orthodox Catholics, and have cultivated relations with some Eastern churches. They stand for the conciliarist tradition together with the divine right of the sacramentally empowered clergy. Thus the Anglican church meets within its own membership the same fundamental issues with which Protestants and Eastern Orthodox Catholics confront each other in church councils and federations.

How has the Anglican and Episcopalian communion held together under these conditions? How combine a sacramental liturgy and hierarchy and an evangelical creed? This was possible because the Anglican church was the creation of political expediency rather than religious passion. Anglicans have no great prophetic figures like Luther and Calvin and the spirit of the Church is nearer Erasmus than either of these. The church was settled by the practical mind of Queen Elizabeth. Nor does this distress Anglicans. They value, by contrast, their very continuity through the Reformation period from times before Hildebrand. This sense of tradition is ever refreshed by Anglican worship, which in Cranmer's *Prayer Book* repeats through the "church year" in the mother tongue much of the best of the product of centuries of Christian worship. This Anglican treasury of the generations has become increasingly the property of other English-speaking Protestant groups. The historic episcopate was similarly retained in Anglicanism through the Reformation as it was in Swedish Lutheranism, and this, too, Anglicans have regarded as a particular value of their heritage, although the majority opinion has always been that the unbroken succession of bishops is not essential for sacramental "validity," as is supposed by the Greek and Roman churches. In other ways, also, Anglicanism has retained, and insisted upon, institutionalist and sacramental forms, while conceding in the Thirty-nine articles that they are Protestant in character, that is, useful but not indispensable to the ministry of God's forgiveness through the church. The Catholic minority, of course, deny this Protestant interpretation. Within this "bridge" church between Protestantism and Catholicism there is thus a wider range of religious opinion and practice than is known to any other. And while the mother church is still intimately associated with the political government of Great Britain, and in many ways insular in character, the English-speaking commonwealth of nations and the United States all know Episcopal churches now linked in world-wide fellowship to Lambeth palace.

Lutherans

Lutheranism, the church of the majority of European Protestants, centered on the countries around the Baltic, is the second great ecclesiastical system of the conservative Reformation. With the closely related thought of Calvinism, Lutheranism stands at the other pole from the optimistic

humanist perspective and the emphasis on man's ethical
and mystical aspiration which have been so pervasive in the
movements so far discussed. Lutheranism sprang from a
profound re-experience of the type of religion eloquently
described by Paul. It was a discovery of healing for the
deep scars of guilt and self-centeredness through a simple
trust in the merciful concern of God. Lutheran piety is still
fed by this warm and joyful appropriation of God's mercy
in Christ perpetually offered. The assurance is independent
of sacramental mediation and is received in the promises of
the Word while men are still deep in their sins. Gratitude
finds release through spontaneous love for our neighbors and
the gospel ethic is confined to private and personal relationships. The state, war, the economic order and social structure are accepted as necessary regulations of human sin to
which the Christian must submit. Unlike Romanism and
Calvinism, there is here a passive resignation akin to the
political and ethical submission of Eastern Orthodoxy. Its
patriarchal conservatism has made Lutheranism too often a
tool of militarism and imperialism. While Luther's first conception of church organization was apparently of the type Calvin so successfully instituted, the accident of circumstance
only strengthened his own tendency to leave such practical
questions to the good will of evangelical princes joyful in
the knowledge of their redemption. The German Lutheran
churches fell permanently into the hands of the political
authorities, with disastrous results down to our own day. The
full life of the Christian community was never freed. There
was, in fact, no real congregational life at all until very
recent times. Scandinavian Lutheranism, by contrast, has had
a healthier life in both respects.

The Lutheran church also became, like the Roman Catholic church, and despite its first prophet, a church of the
clergy. The temptations of clerical authority made them-

selves felt among Lutheran clergy and superintendents. Luther's own theology, particularly his lapse into scholastic absurdities with regard to the Lord's Supper, was not an unmixed blessing. Doctrinal squabbles have marred the history of Lutheranism from the days of the Augsberg Confession to the difficulties of Missouri Synod Lutherans today. Petty Inquisitions have flattered by imitation the abomination of Romanism. "Faith" has tended time and again to retrograde from its religious meaning of trust in a personal God to its scholastic sense of intellectual affirmation of a set of doctrinal propositions. The Word of God, similarly, tended in time to flatten out into the words of the Bible as happened also with Anabaptists and Calvinists. In all these ways evangelical Protestantism has shown itself subject to corruption, while on the other hand, even the Romanism of Trent has never been able to stifle completely the evangelical life in its bosom.

The concentration of Lutheran energies on the deeper religious levels at the expense of morality has had marked influence on the cultural life of Germany. That musical and philosophical leadership which Germany has exercised in the modern world is not unrelated to her Lutheran tradition. No other branch of Christianity in history has made such contributions to music, both directly by its development of liturgical masses, chorales, and the like, and indirectly, by training the whole nation to a high level of musical taste. It was only appropriate that the musical master of European civilization, J. S. Bach, should have found his inspiration and task in the musical interpretation of the emotional depths of "justification by faith." Is there not a similar relationship between German metaphysical preeminence and the intuitive depth of Lutheran piety? In any case Germany has furnished Protestantism with the great bulk of its scholarship and systematic thought.

Presbyterians and Reformed

The third great church and state system of the confessional era was the most ambitious of all in its institutional and ethical goals. Unlike Lutheranism and Anglicanism, the "Reformed" tradition was, at least from the time when Calvin began to mold it, independent in relation to civil government and international in character. Calvin, the Cyprian of the sixteenth century, came the nearest to the construction of an ecumenical, constitutionally governed church catholic of all these heirs of the conciliarist tradition.

The piety of the Reformed churches had already taken on most of its characteristic emphases under Zwingli's leadership in Zurich in the decade before Calvin came to Geneva. It expressed the nervous intelligence, moral discipline and high self-consciousness of the new urban society more than the profound emotional life of the peasant. Both Zwingli and Calvin had good humanist training and came from the influence of Pico, Erasmus, and Lefèvre to that of Luther, and their enthusiasm for the Scriptures always had in it something of the note of humanist revival of the purer streams of antiquity. Yet this humanist view of the Bible as a standard of morality and religious truth was fused with the Lutheran insight that the Bible was the vehicle of the news of God's saving grace. The Lutheran concentration on reconciliation through Christ is broadened in Reformed piety to a more generalized awareness of God's universal sway over all creation. There is less warmth and intimacy with the Redeemer, more of awe and homage to the glory of Creator and Ruler. Old Testament and Catholic motifs blend here in an austerity that is scrupulous against all worship of mere creatures, Virgin, saints, images, relics, natural beauties, for One alone is worthy of worship.

While Luther had wisely restrained the implications of predestination to the joyful assurance of him who is chosen, Calvin, like Aquinas, did not balk at the speculative development which attributes to the one Lord the horrible decree of condemnation of the majority of men. Similarly, Calvin did not guard against the confusion of the Word of God with the words of the Bible as adequately as Luther, and Calvinists have for generations, despite their fear of idolatry, been widely estimated, and too often truly, as Bibliolaters. Which is more preposterous and less evangelical, the declaration of the Vatican Council in 1870 that the bishop of Rome is infallible in his pronouncements on faith and morals, or the declaration of Swiss Calvinists in 1675 that the very grammar and vowel pointings of the Biblical text are divinely certified? The latter, to be sure, never had any standing outside Switzerland. It was Calvin, however, who gave to the Reformation its classical theological statement in one of the masterpieces of world literature, the *Institutes of the Christian Religion*.

More influential than Calvinist theology, however, have been Calvinist ethics and political theory. Calvinism, unlike the separatists, intended to be a church for all the people. It succeeded, moreover, further than any other branch of Christianity has ever done, in making every aspect of community life acknowledge one sovereign Lord. Popular jokes about Puritan "blue-laws" and changing notions of public morality have obscured for many the true significance of the disciplined communities of Geneva, Scotland, Holland, France, England, and New England. We must return to the cultural effects of the Calvinist doctrine of vocation, of church-state relationships, and of political theory. Both the community sense of Americans and their prevailing moralistic utilitarian outlook are parts of our secularized heritage from Geneva via Puritanism, and are still salient traits to observers from authoritarian and individualistic Romanist cultures. American government, similarly, is the best example of that conservative non-equalitarian Calvinist democracy which Troeltsch considers one of the most significant patterns of social and political life in Western history.

The New Trent Religion

It is often said that the Reformation simply substituted an infallible Bible for an infallible Pope, a formula which is incorrect on both counts. The popes were not generally regarded as infallible before the Reformation, and the Reformation did not acknowledge an infallible Bible. The Reformers simply asserted the traditional Christian conception that the Word of God in the Bible must be the last court of resort in the church. They applied this criterion more radically, to be sure, to widespread abuses than had been done before. The fundamental novelty with regard to the problem of authority which the sixteenth century produced was the new and unprecedented decision rendered by the Council of Trent. This was the council which gathered to reorganize the Roman church in defense against the Reformation just four hundred years ago. So radical was its reorganization that one may well ask the modern Romanist, "Where was your church before Trent?" To the dismay of its more sober members, the Council of Trent, for the first time in Christian history, set up "tradition" as of "equal" authority to the Bible. Well might Bishop Ken speak of "the new Trent religion."

The content of this tradition acclaimed as of equal authority with the revelation of God in Christ is variegated. Many elements of popular paganism had pressed their way into the post-Constantinian church and were domesticated as the "veneration" of saints, relics, and particularly the Virgin Mary. Many of the "saints" were local pagan deities and still today, in such places as Latin America, one finds extraordinary fusions of heathenism with a Catholic veneer. The case of the Virgin Mary, however, is most serious, since she has in actual practice replaced Jesus Christ as the mediator between man and God for millions of Roman Catholics everywhere.

The worship of the mother of Jesus was unknown in the early church and first crops up toward the end of the fourth century as a heresy in Thrace and Arabia, where certain women adored the Virgin as a goddess. This was the region where the pagan worship of the "Great Mother" had flourished, and there is much reason to think that modern Romanism with its exaltation of Mary has substantially replaced Jesus Christ by the goddess Cybele. Devotion to Mary has since progressed from this obscure heresy of the fourth century to the decision of the Roman pope in 1854 that it is necessary to salvation for a Christian to believe her to have been free of original sin even from the moment of her conception. The first stage of this development presented the opinion that she remained always virgin, despite the many Biblical references to Jesus' brothers and sisters and the allusion to him as Mary's "first-born son." The testimony of Scripture that all men without exception are sinners seemed confirmed by Mary's confession, only possible to a sinner, of God as her "Savior." The notion spread, nevertheless, that she must have lived a life free from sin, as Augustine urged. By the seventh century her legend had borrowed from Jesus the empty tomb and the assumption of her mortal body into heaven and the "Feast of the Assumption" was established. The crowning glory of the immaculate conception, however, was resisted much longer. The universal testimony of the church for over ten centuries was that Mary was not immaculately conceived. Augustine, Bernard, Thomas Aquinas supported this consensus, together with half a dozen popes who were one day to be discovered to have been infallible. The same logic which made Mary immaculate, as Bernard observed, should apply also to her parents, and her grandparents, and her great grandparents indefinitely. This "superstition," as Thomas Aquinas characterized it, nevertheless has been laid on the consciences of all Romanists in flat defiance of the tradition and consensus of the early church and most of the fathers of the pre-Reformation church, simply on its status as the opinion of a modern pope, who *felt*, as he said, that he was infallible.

Granting, however, that this development of doctrine about Mary is a work of the pious imagination with no historical basis whatever, what harm does it entail? Surely the creative imagination has often been a means of awakening men to the presence of God. And surely none would deny that the cult of Mary has kindled awareness of what we may call the feminine and motherly aspects of God, as well as of the dignity and redemptive power of idealized womanhood. Are not countless paintings of Madonnas to be found in evangelical homes, and are not Ave Marias sung by Protestant choirs? In no evangelical piety, however, is Mary permitted to replace Jesus Christ as the bearer of God's mercy, as she does for millions of Romanists with ecclesiastical approval. The sanction of Rome supports the affirmations of theologians who deny that any man can be saved without the protection of the Virgin, and assert that even God obeys her "command." What a fall is here from the preaching of repentance and the perfect holiness of the Kingdom! The reconciliation brought by Jesus Christ is indissoluble from his known historical character and absolute spiritual and ethical demands. Mary announced no Kingdom of the living God and her historical character neither is nor can be known. Jesus the Christ alone has power to forgive sin, but the cult of Mary is based on the superstition that she can obtain for men release from the *consequences* of sin. This is the fundamental perversion of the gospel which has tainted the adoration of the Virgin and the saints from its inception and against which Protestantism must ever maintain the purity and unequaled authority of God's revelation in Christ. The bishops of Trent placed themselves beside Joe Smith and the Mormons when they exalted this kind of tradition as a new and equal revelation with the gospel.

Among both Mormons and Roman Catholics, fortunately, there are thousands who are content to say simply "I am of Christ."

The history of Tridentine Romanism (that is, the Romanism of Trent) has elucidated the consequences of that fatal error of Trent. Once committed to extra-Biblical tradition as actual revelation, the manifold disagreements within the tradition have pushed Romanists inescapably to the last step, the definition that the final authoritiy and revelation of the church is neither Biblical nor traditional but the mere say-so of the current pope-king. Thus when Pius IX was reproached with the historical fact that tradition witnessed without disagreement for over a thousand years against the infallibility of the pope, for the definition of which he was scheming, he replied, "I am tradition." The same principle was enunciated by Cardinal Manning, whose unscrupulous intrigues were the chief human agency in engineering the infallibility decree through the Vatican Council. "All difficulties from human history," said he, "are excluded by prescription." Lord Acton, the Roman Catholic editor of the *Cambridge Modern History*, defines similarly this postulate of modern Romanism: "The existence of tradition has nothing to do with evidence, and objections taken from history are not valid when contradicted by ecclesiastical decrees. Authority must conquer history."

It is obvious that this rejection of free and honest scholarly inquiry about the history of the Bible and the church makes Romanism opposed on principle and irrevocably to modern science. The most influential devotional work of modern Romanism, Loyola's *Spiritual Exercises,* inculcates the principle "I will believe what seems to me black to be white if the hierarchical church so teaches." In practice this means, as Lord Acton said of that Jesuit party which captured the whole church in 1870, "It not only promotes, it inculcates distinct mendacity and deceitfulness. In certain cases it is made a duty to lie. But those who teach this doctrine do not become habitual liars in other things." There can be no free study or teaching, of history in particular, in Roman Catholic schools or universities. In so far as Roman Catholics penetrate other educational institutions they must and will attempt to censor and silence honest research on these issues. "They [will] at once become irreconcilable enemies of civil and religious liberty," to quote from Lord Acton again. "They will have to profess a false system of morality, and to repudiate literary and scientific sincerity. They will be as dangerous to civilized society in the school as in the state." The widespread Roman Catholic pressure on publishers, newspaper editors, and book dealers, as well as the history of Romanist efforts to expurgate textbooks in the public schools and to tamper with reference works like the *Encyclopaedia Britannica,* are normal and necessary defenses of a system which cannot stand the light of historical science. The fact that Romanist doctrine releases the faithful from the obligation to tell the truth to "heretics" when the interests of the church are at stake explains also many of the startling tactics which have been used by Roman controversialists against Protestant and other non-Romanist historians. The co-operation of uninhibited inquiry and religious faith, of theology and science, is possible only on Protestant territory where all human traditions and institutions stand open both to man's scrutiny and to God's.

Chapter IV

Modern Protestantism

ᖾᖾᖾᖾᖾᖾᖾᖾᖾᖾᖾᖾᖾᖾᖾᖾᖾᖾᖾᖾᖾᖾᖾᖾᖾᖾᖾᖾᖾᖾᖾᖾᖾᖾᖾᖾᖾᖾ

OF THE SIX GREAT FAMILIES OF PROTESTANTISM we have accounted for the origins of three. The great majority of Continental Protestants still belong to either a Lutheran or a Reformed church, and the Church of England still holds a significant proportion of English Protestants. European Protestantism thus contrasts sharply with American Protestantism in the apparent simplicity of its ecclesiastical structure. This simplicity is, to be sure, somewhat deceptive, for the several communions are in fact much divided by political boundaries, even obsolete boundaries. And practically every one of these political divisions of European Protestantism has been transplanted to America. But Europe does not have the denominational complexity in any given locality which is characteristic of America.

As we proceed to the analysis of the remaining Protestant families, it will become apparent that they are not distinctive churches of the Reformation Anglican and Lutheran variety, but belong to a new type of organization, the "denomination." There is less point to a review of their minor individual peculiarities than to a study of denominationalism as a whole, its origins in the English and American Puritan tradition, its secondary effects on the older churches of the Reformation, and its expansion geographically around the world. Then we may profitably consider the changed relations of Protestant Christianity to civilization in this modern age and finally the new ecumenical Protestant discussions, the revived Reformation debates over man's nature and capacities, and over the authority to be yielded to traditional forms and institutions as appointed vehicles of God's mercy to man.

The Denominational Phase

The three remaining major families of Protestantism include the Methodists, the Congregationalists, and the Baptists and Disciples group. All arose since the sixteenth century and in the English-speaking world. Whatever differences they may sense among themselves, moreover, seem unimportant to a foreign observer who sees them for what they are, all members of what we may loosely term the Puritan tradition. Within this tradition we must also include our Presbyterians and many of our Episcopalians as the result of internal changes in their life. While these groups differ on various points, chiefly questions of organization, they all share the basically Calvinist theological tradition of the Thirty-nine Articles and the Westminster Confession, held with varying degrees of fidelity. Even more important, all share the Calvinist ethical tradition of "activist" disciplined effort in state and thought and business for the glory of God. Together they represent by far the most important type of Protestantism in the English-speaking countries, in Australia and New Zealand and Canada as well as England and the United States. They represent in fact the most significant religious force in modern Western civilization, and in particular they are responsible for what Christian discipline and direction have been given to modern democracy and modern economic organization. To understand this achievement, and to grasp the peculiar character of these "denominations" in contrast both to the great church-state systems of the Reformation and to the separate holy communities of the Anabaptists, we must look first to the seventeenth century in England and America.

Puritanism first appeared in the days of William Shakespeare and Queen Elizabeth as a movement for the purification of the Church of England from Catholic practices. Most Puritans remained Anglicans, but some insisted on a truly

Protestant church without tarrying. They formed illegal separatist churches, the ancestors of our present Congregational and Baptist churches. In this they resembled the Anabaptists of the preceding century, but there were differences of fundamental importance. In contrast to Anabaptist pacifism and withdrawal from the world, these radical Puritans cherished rather the Reformed ambition of a Christian state and a Christian community. They sought these goals, however, on the basis of the freedom they admired in Anabaptism, the freedom of the local congregation to determine its own membership and govern its own affairs independently of state regulation. In the period when these radical Puritans governed England by Cromwell's army they demonstrated their hopes. They rejected the Presbyterian state church contemplated by the Westminster Assembly. Yet they firmly intended to make England *more* Christian than she had been or could be under any uniform authoritarianism, Roman Catholic, Anglican, or Reformed. They did not regard ecclesiastical uniformity as necessary for this end, nor even theological uniformity, within certain limits. But Christian conduct and standards in state and community would be sought in dead earnestness. Congregationalists, Baptists, even Quakers, yes, even Presbyterians if they would reconcile themselves to it, could then live side by side in freedom and in common endeavor to build a state and community as Christian as Calvin's Geneva.

The system was of course profoundly modified by the change of political forces in England and especially by the reestablishment of the monarchy and the Anglican Church. England was never again, however, to have a real state church of the earlier type, for she could never again claim more than a fraction of the Protestant population for the preferred church. She was forced to a compromise with the views of what were now become "Non-conformists" and the theory of religious liberty was formulated by the liberal

Calvinist John Locke. The American colonies were to be
the scene of the first enduring experiment in this Puritan
program of free churches in a Christian community. From
Baptist Rhode Island and Quaker Pennsylvania and New
Jersey the conception penetrated into the Calvinist Presbyterian and Congregational and Anglican colonies, pre-
paring the soil for religious freedom in the several state
constitutions and at length the new national constitution.*

Reasons of economic and political expediency also made
themselves felt, especially among the lawyers and statesmen,
but it was this Puritan religious respect for the freedom of
conscience which made the masses of church people amenable. Religious indifference played a role in the separation
of church and state in America, but a minor one, and the
contrast is sharp with Roman Catholic and even Lutheran
countries, where separation has normally come, where it has
come, by a bitter struggle *against* the church. In the Puritan
conception, separation meant a division of powers, for the
greater freedom of the churches, within a community of
common Protestant views and standards. The overwhelming
majority of American Christians, it must be remembered,
were of this Puritan tradition at the formative epoch of our
national life. The four largest religious bodies in the United
States then were the Congregationalists, Presbyterians, Bap-

---

* Recent Roman Catholic writers have won more credit for their political sympathies than for their historical accuracy in claiming toleration
in early Maryland for Rome. The Maryland charter was granted by a
Protestant government to a Roman Catholic proprietor. Had Baltimore
not tolerated Protestants in the colony his charter could never have endured, especially since the colonists, who were from the beginning predominantly Protestant, had the power of vetoing his legislation. Romanism
must not be held responsible for arrangements forced on Catholics by
circumstances, against the teaching of the Papal Court. There is much
less basis for the legend, widely disseminated by people who should know
better, like Cardinal Hayes and John A. Ryan, that Jefferson's ideas were
inspired by the Venerable Bellarmine. No more should have been heard
of this after David S. Schaff's *The Bellarmine-Jefferson Legend,* 1928.

tists, and Anglicans—and the last predominantly Puritan Anglicans. A generation or so would add the Methodists to this list. These groups, with the Quakers, set the American pattern of religion in state and society. Continental Protestants were few and isolated by language barriers, while Roman Catholics were wholly insignificant.

We must return to the very important relation between Puritanism and religious liberty and democracy. Here our concern is rather to define this new type of organization, the "denomination," and its implications for internal Protestant relations. The very term implies that the group referred to is but one member of a family with a common faith. No "denomination" claims, as did the Lutherans, Reformed, Anglicans, and Romanists of the Reformation century, that the whole state and society should be submitted to its ecclesiastical regulation. Yet the denominations all recognize a responsibility for that more inclusive community. Each expects to co-operate in freedom and mutual respect with other denominations of Protestant Christians for the same truth and the same obedience. The practical implications and the difficulties of this new type of church organization have been making themselves felt increasingly during the last century. It has become apparent, for example, that denominational multiplicity is a serious confusion and handicap in predominantly non-Christian cultures, as in Asia. In the West, similarly, the rise of non-Christian quasi-religious movements, such as Marxism or nationalism, put the denominational pattern of Protestant cultural and political expression to a similar strain. The pattern is challenged even by the presence of a large Christian contingent who do not accept the toleration involved, such as the Roman Catholics, who scheme endlessly for special privilege before the law or in spite of it. American Protestantism in our generation must reconsider this whole system of church-state relationships, especially as it relates to public education and the morals of state actions. The pattern historically assumes all through society a common Protestant outlook, which no longer exists.

This "denominational" structure of Protestant life has been fully developed only in America, where churches of other traditions than the Puritan group, such as Lutherans, Anglicans, and Roman Catholics, have been forced to adapt themselves to it, if in the last case only provisionally. In Europe, however, similar pressures have made themselves felt, working within the traditional state-church pattern of the confessional age.

A new movement sprang up in the late seventeenth and eighteenth century for the cultivation of a type of separatist fellowship *within* the churches. Little prayer meetings and reading circles of "pietists" gathered to share religious experience and strengthen one another in moral discipline. Like the Anabaptists, they wished only "converted" members. But again, as with the radical Puritans, they did not intend to go the whole way of non-violent, world-renouncing religion. They were willing to submit to political authority, and if necessary, take part in it. And since political authority insisted on the state church in Germany, most of them stayed within that. They had a carelessness about rigid official theology, however, and fine points of churchmanship, for these things were all externals.

The "denominational" theory of a common Protestantism was here developed by Count Zinzendorf, who was to be the founder of the chief new denomination of this movement on the Continent. His intent, however, was to organize a fellowship to work within the existing communions like the early "Society of Friends," and in particular within the Lutheran, the Unity of Brethren, and the Reformed communions. Each of these three constituted a "mode" of expressing in piety, thought, and organization, the common Christian experience. He deprecated all proselyting from

one to another and labored passionately for the deepening
and vitalizing of all. The "Moravians," however, became
in time a separate denomination despite themselves. Their
present-day membership is not large, but their great significance has been their influence on the larger established
churches. The Moravians were the founders of Protestant
missions, catching up this pattern of personal evangelism
from the Anabaptists, in contrast to the state-supported missions of the authoritarian churches. The Moravians were
really a Protestant order, of which every member was on call
for evangelistic service.

A similar development occurred within Anglicanism under
the leadership of the Wesley brothers. The "Methodists,"
too, were to be a society of convinced Christians, living in
close fellowship and discipline, but still within the Anglican
framework, and supporting the government in war and
peace. And, like the Moravians, who had a strong influence
on him, Wesley claimed a comprehensiveness which gloried
in transcending dogmatic and liturgical boundaries. Predestination and "perfectionism" were not important enough
to keep Christians apart. His view of the church as a redemptive community was very high, but that church was not
to be identified with one uniform institution or theology.
Like the German pietists, he was inclined to the Anabaptist
remnant theory of church history, tracing an apostolic succession through more "heretics" than bishops. He could not
find that heresy and schism were Scriptural sins at all but
suspected they "were invented merely to deprive mankind
of the benefit of private judgment and liberty of conscience."
Clearly we are already far from the Reformers and yet these
men were the most passionate Christians of their century.
The objective revelation and redeeming action of God were
clearly held in view, but the institutional church and its
creeds and doctrine were become merely instrumental, rather

than divinely instituted themselves. The sine qua non was
the experience of reconciliation with God in a Christian
fellowship, however organized.

This Moravian and Methodist interpretation of Christianity found its systematic theoretician at the turn of the
nineteenth century in Friedrich Schleiermacher, the most
influential Protestant theologian since Luther and Calvin.
Refusing to proceed in scholastic fashion from the authorized
creeds and confessions of the church, Schleiermacher began
with the religious experience of the Christian fellowship and
analyzed its character and implications. This concentration
on the verifiable facts of Christian experience, rather than on
inherited theological formulations, coincided with the empirical method which had won such prestige in the natural
sciences. In essence, however, it was simply the Anabaptist-
Moravian perspective, rounded out historically and philo-
sophically and adjusted to the rising respect for the national
community and culture as goods in their own right. Men
like Coleridge and Robertson in England, or Bushnell in
America, mark much the same turning point in Protestant
thinking. The last generation or so, to be sure, has been
troubled by the tendency of this method of theology to de-
generate into mere psychological description. A corrective
emphasis is now apparent on the objective historical revelation of God as the basis of all "religious experience," and
on the problem of the truth of the varying descriptions based
on such experience.

Within the churches of nineteenth century Europe the
Methodist and Moravian type of religion appeared in the
form of "evangelical" awakenings in Scandinavia, Germany,
Switzerland, France, Holland, England, Scotland, within
Lutheran, Reformed, and Anglican traditions. And here
again the Puritan concern for freedom of religion from legal
restrictions made itself felt. The thirties and forties of the
last century saw an epidemic of separations of "free

churches" from the state among European cousins of the
Puritans. In none of these cases was the whole church involved persuaded of the necessity of the step, and all of
them resulted consequently in the erection of new free
churches beside continuing state churches, in Scotland, Holland, France, Switzerland, Germany. The century since,
however, has seen, on the whole, vindication of the essential
position of those who "went out," even in the minds of
those who stayed in the establishments. This shift has made
possible organizational reunions in our own day, such as the
reunited Church of Scotland. This characteristic Calvinist
concern for the independence of the church from the state,
however, has not been combined, as in America, with the
problem of a multiplicity of free churches in one locality.
And Lutheranism and Anglicanism have been much less
exercised by this movement for religious liberty on the part
of the church.

Evangelization of the Nations

The Methodist revival, however, to return to that movement, was more than the cultivation of pietist brotherhoods,
it was a great preaching mission like that of the Franciscans
in the thirteenth century. It was timed so as to catch the
new barbarian invasions from within, the masses of laborers
huddled in the warrens of the early industrial revolution,
without roots or traditions or stake in society. Here was the
greatest home missions campaign Protestantism had seen,
when a dignified Oxford don found himself so consumed with the news of the Kingdom that he would force
himself to preach in the fields or streets or wherever the
people were. In almost the same years the unchurched and
turbulent frontiersmen of America were swept by a similar
"Great Awakening," similarly interdenominational in character. These revivals were to be regularly recurrent in both

Europe and America in the next century and a half which
was to see the population of these areas increase about three
times, far exceeding the capacities of the existing churches.

The present preeminence of the Methodist denomination
as the largest Protestant church in the United States is due
chiefly to the effectiveness of Methodist circuit-riders and
evangelists on the fluid American frontier. The more cultured and ecclesiastically proper Presbyterians, Congregationalists, and Anglicans, who had once seemed destined to
dominate religious America, could not compete over the
Alleghenies with the less inhibited Methodist and Baptist
evangelists. The two latter denominations won the lion's
share on the frontier and give a characteristic tone now to
American Protestantism as a whole. The Disciples and
"Christians" likewise arose out of these frontier revivals in
the Puritan tradition and today may be grouped for all practical and analytical purposes with the Baptists.

This intense evangelistic concern of the Moravian and
Methodist type was not confined to Europeans, either in the
homeland or in America or the British Dominions. All the
great Reformation churches—Anglican, Lutheran, and Reformed—were converted, with some initial resistance, to this
missionary responsibility. All sorts of missionary "societies"
arose, which were in themselves examples of the new type
of voluntary fellowship, and in their practice overseas carried on with an independence of state sponsorship which
was something new in the whole history of Christian expansion since Constantine. Eastern Orthodox missions in Asia
and Roman Catholic ventures in the French and Italian
colonies were much more closely related to political imperialism in the nineteenth century than were the Protestant
missions.

This Protestant movement was one of the greatest geo-
graphical expansions of Christian history. That branch of
the faith which was, up to the end of the eighteenth cen-

tury, almost entirely the religion of Northern and Western Europe, became, in four or five generations more, solidly rooted in every continent and major people. While still numbering less than half of all Christians, evangelical Protestantism has been steadily gaining in proportion to the two other branches of Christendom since the sixteenth century. And in these centuries it has made the greatest impact on the societies and cultures it has touched of all branches of the Church. The sweep of this movement may be recalled by a listing of some famous names: Carey of India, Judson of Burma, Moffat and Livingstone of Africa, Morrison of China, Martyn in the Moslem Middle East, and figures in our own day like Kagawa, Augustine Ralla Ram, T. Z. Koo, D. T. Niles who testify that this lend-lease traffic is increasingly moving in both directions. The whole balance of Protestantism is shifting, with the Asiatic leadership rapidly occupying a full equality with the European and North American contingents, while the extraordinarily rapid growth of Protestantism in a country like Brazil points to major changes in Latin America. And what this will mean for the life and thought of the whole defies prediction.

The Younger Evangelical Churches of Japan, India, Africa, the East Indies, Brazil, Argentina, Mexico, the Philippines are largely the heirs of this free and mobile Protestantism with its valuation of an actual fellowship of believers and new personal life over dogmatic and ecclesiastical correctness. The overwhelming non-Christian majorities constantly confronting the Christian communities with awkward decisions on social, ethical, philosophical, and religious issues have also constrained the Younger Churches to consolidations over traditional confessional differences. Here was one of the two or three most important forces in the drive to ecumenical Protestantism of the last one hundred years. There was a new sense of the church as a God-given society, but a sense which similarly deprecated the denominations as most inadequate expressions of that "church." Both from within and without, from religious, theological, financial, and political factors came the pressure to consolidate denominations. The Church of Christ in China was the most comprehensive Christian union which had yet occurred. The Church of Christ in Japan was even more so, but being partly constrained by a pagan government it is not yet clear whether its unity is enduring. Indian Protestantism presses relentlessly on the home offices of related denominations and seems determined to achieve that union of Anglicans and full Protestants which defies negotiation in the West. Asia has no time for ecclesiastical disorganization which once represented serious religious or theological division but now represents only inertia.

Christianity and Modern Civilization

Another major motif which distinguishes the last two and one half centuries of Protestant life from the confessional age and the middle ages is a new attitude toward civilization. Here again there were beginnings in the suppressed currents of the Reformation. Just as the denominational organization of modern Protestantism in "free churches" embodies elements of the Anabaptist witness, so the humanist confidence in the fundamental goodness of the natural man and his cultural expressions has deeply infiltrated the life even of churches descended from Calvin and Luther. The asceticism and other-worldliness of both the Reformation and the Counter-reformation have yielded in a variety of ways to a positive and even uncritical attitude toward what used to be called "the world." In religious thought, Protestant and Catholic, this development can be traced in the increasing emphasis on human effort, moral or devotional, in the religious life. But the tendency can be read without theological subtleties in the social attitudes and ethics of the churches.

The acceptance of a positive attitude toward political and economic and cultural achievements for their own sake displayed itself in various ways in the different communions and countries. Lutherans, for example, who had been taught to submit themselves to the constituted authorities as a punishment for their sin, imperceptibly found themselves, under the impact of nineteenth century nationalism, serving the state and the German princes for an indiscriminate glory of God and nation. The modern nation-state in many ways is a substitute for the church-state of the Reformation, claiming a right to govern every aspect of life toward one end. Its quasi-religious character first became evident in the French Revolution and the resultant Napoleonic wars. Altar and liturgy, hymns, holy days and martyrs, mystical devotion and fanatical crusades were all adopted at that time for the purposes of the new type of community and state. The tone differed somewhat in Roman Catholic France or Italy from Lutheran Germany, but the same type of synthesis took place. All of these countries were more military and less concerned for responsible liberty than the English-speaking peoples. What democratic elements were to be found emphasized equality rather than liberty, and more readily adjusted themselves to absolute rule, monarchical or totalitarian, Roman Catholic or Lutheran. In these new political religions the inherited forms of Christianity were retained, animated more and more by an essentially pagan spirit, but so gradually that masses of people were not aware that they had passed from one faith to another.

The Reformed tradition, international from the beginning, and often denied political expression as a minority group, displayed less tendency to idealize national states or monarchies. Much of the political activity of the Reformed

peoples, however, had gone into the struggle for constitutional limitations on absolutism and for popular participation
in government, especially in the free church phase of Reformed life. In England and America, in France and Scotland, the reformed and free church tradition has felt itself
the champion of democracy and political freedom and has
been tempted to identify these with Christianity, or to substitute them for it. In the English-speaking countries, nationalism has usually been liberal and humanitarian in spirit
and is so still to a degree in that "American faith" which
mingles democracy, free enterprise, a high color-conscious-
ness, and patriotic pride with a somewhat perfunctory
acknowledgment of God. As asceticism relaxed, similarly,
the economic vocation which the Calvinist and Puritan pur-
sued for the glory of God and the mortification of his flesh
tended to be transmuted into a simple acceptance of the
good of production for the sake of production. This was the
process which set free enterprise beside democracy as an
equivalent or substitute for Christianity for many.

We must not, however, read our own situation back into
these centuries. This synthesis of Christianity and civilization was based on a genuine faith in a good Creator, and in
the harmony of the universe designed by him. Men who
served nation first could trust that God would look to the
harmonizing of national interests. Business men could look
out each for his own profit in the confidence that so the
greatest good of the community would be served. The fact
that we have largely lost this confidence of the eighteenth
and nineteenth centuries in God's automatic harmonization
of conflicting endeavors should not make us doubt the sincerity of those who held it. For several generations God *did*
provide at least a rough harmony and men could serve at once
and with integrity what we now see to be rival gods in our
generation. The final sanction for this harmony was the
idea of progress, the notion that this earnest striving of men

for their several interests would be rewarded in the nature of things by a future of justice and plenty, a kind of secularized version of the fulfillment of the Kingdom. This faith reached its culmination in the United States between the Civil War and 1929. While the old alliance of Protestantism with economic and political liberalism and nationalism is now come to an impasse where men must choose, for long it was a possible synthesis for Christian ethics, perhaps as good as Thomas Aquinas' or John Calvin's in their day.

We cannot, however, exculpate Protestantism, or Roman Catholicism or Orthodoxy either, from a widespread default of Christian obedience in these centuries in practical ethical matters like politics and business, even among those most rigid in intellectual orthodoxy. There has been no great popular rising out of a new vision of the Kingdom such as took place in each of the sixteenth and seventeenth and eighteenth centuries. Or rather, there has been such a rising, but it came outside the churches and in large measure in opposition to the churches, even while living largely off their neglected resources. The rising was, of course, Marxist socialism, a Judaeo-Christian heresy which succeeded to the role Christianity had earlier played in forming the ethical and social aspirations of men just because the churches had betrayed their trust. The success of Marxism is the measure of Christian failure.

The noble line of reformers and philanthropists from the seventeenth century Quakers down through the Methodist and Evangelical awakenings and the nineteenth century must never be forgotten. We need mention only John Howard and Elizabeth Fry in prison reform; Woolman and Benezet, Wilberforce, Clarkson, and Finney and their tireless fight against Negro slavery; Lord Shaftesbury and Rauschenbusch with their concern for child labor and factory legislation. Similar names, less well known in America, could be listed for France and Germany and Switzerland and other coun-

tries. There has been a vast and measureless outpouring of
Christian philanthropy and reform of social abuses which
has changed the whole tone of industrial society. And yet
even this movement failed to preach the full gospel of God's
Reign. This was a matter of snatching brands from the burn-
ing, of reforming individuals or specific abuses, but never
of preaching the judgment and redemption of the living
God to the whole order of society. Christians were content,
overwhelmingly, with liberal or democratic capitalism and
let the voice of truth and prophecy die out from among them.
It was the Marxists who dared, like Nathan, to cry "Thou
art the man!"; to call injustice and exploitation by its name
and to preach the confidence that the power of history was
a power for justice even if the last days would bring trials
and wars. And by its superior honesty and moral clarity
Marxism won great masses of the disinherited, particularly
in Lutheran Germany. Romanist countries were more re-
sistant and Calvinist and Puritan peoples were nearly im-
mune to this heresy. The relative ethical vigor of the various communions in modern society was thus illustrated
again.

Today it is the post-Marxian theologians who are giving
Protestantism its clearest intellectual and ethical orientation
in our revolutionary generation. Out of the Swiss Christian
socialists have come Brunner and Barth and Thurneysen and
out of the German, Tillich. In America Reinhold Niebuhr's
Moral Man and Immoral Society was the herald of a new
social realism and a new theological depth. It is only out
of such critical analysis of our secular civilization that the
crumbling synthesis of Protestantism with middle-class culture can be interpreted and its emancipation achieved. In
America the revolution is only beginning and the churches
are uncertain and hesitant. These Protestant prophets are
warning us, however, that this is indeed a time of the breaking of nations, when the whole social and intellectual struc-

ture of Protestant peoples is threatened, and the church must listen again for the voice of the sovereign God and disengage itself from all compromising associations with idolatries.

Polarities within Evangelical Catholicism

In this tension between the claims of modern civilization and the search for the Kingdom of God lies the occasion for some of the deepest present tensions within Protestantism. The lines are drawn sharply between those of liberal, humanistic, and optimistic views about modern civilization and social reform, and those who are suspicious of the natural man and all his works, however idealistic. The debate between Luther and Erasmus on human capacities for good is resumed. At present this debate is umpired by the Atlantic. Of all the world's Protestants it is the Americans who are now most Erasmian. Two generations ago our believing forefathers were utterly scandalized at the worldly ideas which came out of Lutheran German institutions and professors. Today the shoe is on the other foot, and the Continentals are hard put to it to discover anything specifically Christian in the humanitarian idealism of liberal American Protestants. A wettened finger seems to indicate a change in the wind over the prairies, however, and another decade may see a very different situation. In any case the individualism of the last few generations seems gone before a recovery of the Reformation sense that God is Lord over every relationship and order of our lives.

The last generation or so has also seen a great revival of the Reformation and conciliar awareness of the visible church universal. This recovery has found institutional expression in the so-called "ecumenical" movement, an *evangelical* catholicism, now co-ordinated in the manifold activities of the World Council of Churches. To an historian of Christianity this institutional consolidation of Protestantism, and the rapprochement between Protestantism and Orthodox Catholicism, is probably the most striking development of the first half of the twentieth century. At times it has seemed that this movement, like the Oxford Movement of the last century, was an enthusiasm of the clergy alone, if not merely of ecclesiastical globe-trotters, but the second World War proved it to be sustained by a deep and fresh awareness among the laity of the essential oneness of Christ's body everywhere, across all military and cultural frontiers. Just as the leaders of this movement were able to bring together representatives from the recently warring peoples after the first world war, and just as representatives of the Younger Churches actually at war were able to worship together at Madras, so in our day the fellowship and trust of Christians is almost the sole channel of healing among the shattered peoples of Europe. And in all the great assemblies of the church universal in the last generation, at Stockholm, Jerusalem, Lausanne, Oxford, Edinburgh, and Madras, the basis and reality of union was found, not in theological or ethical discussion, but in common adoration, in the memorable services of worship when the "communion of saints" became actuality.

We have already mentioned two of the pressures which have contributed to this ecumenical assembling. The first was the urgency of the Younger Churches, which made itself felt through the International Missionary Council and today supplies a large proportion of the most devoted and intelligent leadership. A second concern has been the increasing awareness of the churches in the last two or three generations of their inadequate social and ethical witness in the modern world. It was this concern in particular which led to co-operation in various parts of the Protestant world of the type of the American Federal Council of Churches. The first international expression was at the Stockholm Conference in 1925, and there the Protestant and Eastern Orthodox churches united on a solemn confession of guilt and unfaithfulness. No one with a vivid sense of the widespread refusal of eighteenth and nineteenth century Protestantism to accept responsibility for the salvation of society will call this a trifling achievement.

A third contributing movement in this ecumenical tide has been the particular emphasis of Christian students. Even in the nineteenth century the new evangelical comprehensiveness was foreshadowed in the interdenominational student groups, the Young Men's Christian Association, the Young Women's Christian Association, the Christian Endeavor, the Student Volunteer Movement, and the Student Christian Movement. In such organizations as these, students of various denominations learned to think and worship and work together as Christians, and in many cases as more intense Christians than they had been in their denominational compartments. It has often been remarked how large a proportion of the leaders of the ecumenical movement, men like the Archbishops Soederblom and William Temple, passed their apprenticeship in the Student Christian movement. Those who try to live and think as Christians in the modern university find themselves like Younger Churchmen, on a frontier of paganism and secularism where the luxury of denominational division is too expensive and too dangerous to be retained.

Actual organic consolidation of Protestant denominations seems agonizingly protracted, yet over thirty mergers have been consummated in this generation. The most striking of these in America is the formation of the United Church of Canada of Methodist, Congregational, and Presbyterian churches, an institutional recognition of the essential unity of the Puritan group of denominations. The same groups are negotiating for similar ventures in other parts of the British Commonwealth of Nations and like possibilities have been discussed now and again in the United States.

Such institutional reform, however, advisable as much of
it undoubtedly is, is not the most important aspect of the
ecumenical recovery of the church universal. Neither international conferences nor the consolidation of denominational
administration are worth the effort unless they contribute to
the religious realization of the local congregation that it is
simply the local representative of Christ's worldwide fellowship. Wherever that realization is strong enough to shake
the patterns of class and national and racial pride in a community, there the ecumenical movement finds fulfillment,
whatever the administrative superstructure may be. There
is evidence that this realization of universal Christian sol-
idarity is still imperfect. When the delegates to the ecumenical conference of Christian youth at Amsterdam on the
eve of the last war were asked whether they felt that the
ecumenical vision was preached and understood in their
parish churches, the reply was a resounding "No"! There
are even reports that men and women brought to Christianity by the vision of its universal fellowship have turned
in despair from Protestant churches to Romanism, in the
hope that national provincialism and parish-mindedness
would there be corrected by an international church government.

The struggle for the recovery of the Reformation concern
for the visible Christian community as a universal society
raises again polarities similar to those of the reviving theological debate over human nature and civilization. As we
have seen, the Anglican, Lutheran, and Reformed or Presbyterian churches have been penetrated in many ways by
elements of left-wing thought and practice, yet they still
share a sense for historical continuity, for the sacramental uses of liturgy, theology, and church government as
means of grace which is largely foreign to the left-wing
tradition. American Protestantism is dominated by the latter.
About half of its churches are congregational in character,

without strong bonds to the past or to each other, without resources in liturgical tradition or theology to temper the lapses of inspiration of its preachers. The clergy, to a considerable degree, are lay preachers so far as theological education is concerned. These churches can often be aroused to co-operation in ethical activity, but for the specifically ecclesiastical side of the ecumenical revival they have little understanding. When they do develop a philosophical theology it characteristically lacks a sense of history and of historical community and runs to a naturalism more or less tinged with Christian feeling and standards. The whole American development has largely transferred the religious and ethical vitality of Protestantism to religious and ethical groups outside the ecclesiastical structure. The bare bones of church institutions and authorities are often regarded as somehow necessary but antiquated and unlovely and still potentially dangerous. One might almost describe American Protestantism in its dominant patterns as an experiment in Christianity with a minimum of the church.

A widespread new interest in worship and liturgy and religious art, however artificial and flossy it often seems, is a symptom of a sense of loss, and parallels a new interest in the theology which was earlier considered dispensable. It is to be hoped that the left-wing Baptists and Congregationalists and Methodists and Disciples will continue their protests against all pretensions to "right" order and "valid" sacraments in the assurance that the grace of God is bound to no institutions or levitical brotherhoods. There is much for them to learn, on the other hand, of what the visible church should be which has been better preserved by Episcopalians, Lutherans, and Presbyterians. The present tendency is indicated by the transition Harry Emerson Fosdick describes from his earlier view that "we make the church" to his present conviction, "the church makes us." Out of this discussion, which will also be carried on across the Atlantic with European Protestantism and across the Pacific with the Younger Churches, may emerge a more comprehensive synthesis of the insights of the varied strands of the Reformation movement. The ecumenical rising may then see a new Protestantism capable of uniting the truth of the Anabaptist witness with the high conception of the church held by Calvin, Cranmer, or Luther.

Let us now turn from this outline of the Protestant movement with its internal tensions and varieties to a survey of those convictions and insights which have defined the common heritage.

Part 2

Protestant Principles

Chapter V

Protestant Principles: 1. The Sole Headship of Jesus Christ

VIEWING THE REFORMATION and the four succeeding Protestant centuries together, we may describe five enduring motifs of Protestant life and thought.

Christ's Intrinsic Authority

The fundamental principle of the Reformation is perhaps most eloquently stated by an Eastern Orthodox writer, Dostoievsky, in the words of his Grand Inquisitor, the voice of the Roman Counter-reformation. The story, it will be recalled, is laid in Spain, in Seville, in the most terrible time of the Inquisition, when fires were lighted every day to the glory of God. And there in his infinite mercy Christ came down among men, down to the hot pavement of the southern town in which, on the day before, almost a hundred heretics had *ad majorem gloriam Dei* been burnt by the cardinal, the Grand Inquisitor.* He was recognized by all and surrounded by worshipers and children crying "Hosanna," while the crowd wept and kissed the earth under his feet. The blind recovered their sight once more, and the dead were raised before all the people. And then, suddenly, came the guards of the Inquisition, who laid hands on him, and in deathlike silence, led him away. In the blackness of that night the

---

* *The Brothers Karamazov*, Part II, Book V, Chapter V. From the edition published by the Crown Press, New York.

cardinal visited Christ in his cell and rebuked him for dar-
ing to bring even there his gospel of evangelical freedom,
promising to burn him the next day as the worst of heretics.

Thou didst desire man's free love, that he should follow
thee freely, enticed and taken captive by thee. In place of the
ancient rigid law, man must hereafter with free heart decide
for himself what is good and what is evil, having only thy
image before him as his guide. . . . Thou didst crave faith
freely given, not based on miracle. Thou didst crave for free
love and not the base raptures of the slave before the might
that has overawed him for ever. . . . The freedom of their faith
was dearer to thee than anything in those days fifteen hundred
years ago.

How is the weak soul to blame that it is unable to receive
such terrible gifts? And if for the sake of the bread of Heaven
thousands and tens of thousands shall follow thee, what is
to become of the millions and tens of thousands of millions
of creatures who will not have the strength to forego the
earthly bread for the sake of the heavenly? Canst thou have
come simply to the elect and for the elect? But if so, it is a
mystery and we cannot understand it. And if it is a mystery, we
too have a right to preach a mystery, and to teach them that
it's not the free judgment of their hearts, not love that matters,
but a mystery which they must follow blindly even against
their conscience. So we have done. We have corrected thy
work and founded it upon *miracle, mystery,* and *authority.* We
shall deceive them again, for we will not let thee come to us
again. That deception will be our suffering, for we shall be
forced to lie. Why hast thou come now to hinder us? And
why dost thou look silently and searchingly at me with thy
mild eyes? Be angry. I don't want thy love, for I love thee not.

Listen. We are not working with thee, but with *him.* . . .
Just eight centuries ago* we took from him what thou didst
reject with scorn, that last gift he offered thee. We took from
him Rome and the sword of Caesar, and proclaimed ourselves

---

* cf. above, pages 41 and following.

sole rulers of the earth, though hitherto we have not been able to complete our work. But whose fault is that? We shall triumph and shall be Caesars, and then we shall plan the universal happiness of man—that is, some one to worship, some one to keep his conscience, and some means of uniting all in one unanimous and harmonious ant-heap. We shall tell them that every sin will be expiated, if it is done with our permission, and they will have no secrets from us. And they will be glad to believe our answer, for it will save them from the great anxiety and terrible agony they endure at present in making a free decision for themselves. What I say to thee will come to pass and our dominion will be built up. Tomorrow thou shalt see that obedient flock who at a sign from me will hasten to heap up the hot cinders about the pile on which I shall burn thee for coming to hinder us. For if anyone has ever deserved our fires, it is thou. Tomorrow I shall burn thee. I have spoken.

We recall also how the story ended, how the Inquisitor waited some time for the prisoner to answer him, longing for him to say something, however bitter and terrible. But "he suddenly approached the old man in silence and softly kissed him. That was all his answer. The old man shuddered, his lips moved. He went to the door, opened it, and said to Him: 'Go, and come no more . . . come not at all, never, never!' "

We may be permitted to emphasize the issue of this dialogue between the voice of the Reformation and the voice of Tridentine Catholicism, even at the risk of pedantry. The Reformation rests simply on the figure of Christ as accessible to all men in the gospel, a Christ who needs no recommendations, no credentials, who can be trusted by the power of the Spirit to evoke recognition and the love of free men. This is not simply the "right of private judgment." Every man must, to be sure, even if in "great anxiety and terrible agony," make a free and responsible decision for himself.

But it is God who entices and takes him captive in Christ,
God in the figure of Christ, and God illumining the responsive mind and heart. "No man can say that Jesus is Lord but
by the Holy Spirit." This is, if you will, the direct access
of the believer to God, without patented ecclesiastical inter-
mediaries, but it is no subjectivistic mysticism. This is a
faith in the sufficient force of revelation in history, Jesus
Christ, unique, indispensable, self-authenticating. The
"elect" who receive such a "terrible" gift do always seem to
be a minority among men. And the meaning of the incom-
plete lives of those tens of thousands of millions of creatures
who do not receive this gift is indeed a mystery.

The humanitarian and, in some ways, noble motive of
Tridentine Catholicism is also emphasized by Dostoievsky.
It is founded, to be sure, on a lack of faith in God's disclosure of himself, and in his ability to present himself con-
vincingly to men. Lacking faith in the living God, Tridentine Romanism proposes various social and intellectual
devices to coerce men to a degree of submission to the institutional church. These devices are largely prefigured in
Plato, who likewise had lost all faith in the self-authentica-
tion of justice, goodness, and truth to the mass of men.
Plato's republic was to be governed by a clergy of philoso-
pher-kings, with the military and police powers of the state
at their disposal, and education and the arts subjected to
their careful censorship. The whole structure would be
maintained by a "noble lie," an "expedient falsehood," a
bogus revelation, lending a divine sanction to clerical authority. By such means might be achieved a uniform and disciplined religious society, a "unanimous and harmonious ant-
heap" such as the unaided truth of God has never produced,
and such as great masses of men unquestionably prefer to
the terrible responsibilities of making up their own minds on
the intrinsic authority of Jesus Christ.

His Life and Teaching

For all Protestants, in contrast, the focus of God's Word, God's purpose and character, has always centered on Jesus Christ in his whole significance and in the context of history before and since. What are we to say about this crisis and culmination of the disclosure of God's intention? Of Jesus' life history, of what he did and where and in what sequence, we know considerably less than we once thought we did when we believed it possible to extract a chronology and an itinerary of Jesus' apostolate from the Gospels. Historical scholarship can state the established facts about the career of Jesus in about half a page. We know considerably more than ever before, on the other hand, about the cultural movements, the religious ideas, the political and economic pressures which in so many ways determined the content of Jesus' mentality and the external course of his destiny. This kind of knowledge, however, is only general and in some degree establishes chiefly the alien, indigestible, transitory cultural peculiarities of Jesus. Jesus' conceptions of demons and of the imminent end of the world, for example, are a difficulty for many. And yet from this strange and partly alien prophet there come to us the unmistakable, authoritative tones of the eternal Christ of God.

Our conception of the eternal Christ is thus indissolubly connected with the personality of the historical Jesus. And we have sufficient records of the teaching and human relations of Jesus, even though no specific saying can be certainly claimed as precisely his, to establish a highly distinctive and unforgettable personality. The large part of the religious and ethical teachings of the first three gospels is surely his in substance, and while it had been rearranged for the uses of the church even before its writing by the evangelists, much of the form of the teaching is little changed. In these

stories and impressions there come clear certain features of
a religious personality without a counterpart in world history. In this "wine-bibber and glutton," this friend of children and of women, this quick anger and this gift of tears,
this earthy man with the raciness and freshness of the poor
in his humor, here is a humanity and a warmth which the
ascetics and moralists and mystics of religious history cannot
match. Buddha, Socrates, Mohammed, Confucius, Plotinus,
—none was so lovable or so loved as he. Here also was the
gentle strength, the extraordinary sanity and sensitivity required to leave behind a trail of cures among the neurotic
and demon-ridden, the psychosomatically disturbed so common in that hysterical atmosphere of Palestine in the decades
before the last crazy uprising against Rome. And yet whoever pitched his demands with such reckless absoluteness?
The single-mindedness and renunciation required in the
Sermon on the Mount and the parables in the middle of
Luke are terrible and ruthless. "Love your enemies and
pray for those who persecute you." This in an occupied
country seething with revolt! "Give to the man who begs
from you." "Whoever strikes you on the right cheek, turn
the other to him as well." "Anyone who even looks with
lust at a woman has committed adultery with her already in
his heart." "Do not trouble about what you are to eat and
drink in life, nor about what you are to put on your body."
"If anyone comes to me and does not hate his father and
mother and wife and children and brother and sister, aye
and his own life, he cannot be a disciple of mine . . . so with
everyone of you who will not part with all his goods—he
cannot be a disciple of mine." "You must be perfect, as
your father in heaven is perfect." Who else has ever dared
to conceive of human life as having these possibilities, save
as he has learned of them from these lips? There is no other
such absolute program of moral goodness in human history;
this is the ultimate, the demand of perfection, and no higher

can be conceived. If God wills the active holiness of men, this is the authentic vision.

And yet again, all this comes not in the tone of one laying down unbearable standards, but as a comfort and deliverance, an announcement of a great new release, proclaimed by its messenger in his first reported sermon:

> The spirit of the Lord is upon me:
> for he has consecrated me to preach the gospel to the
> poor,
> he has sent me to proclaim release for captives
> and recovery of sight for the blind,
> to set free the oppressed,
> to proclaim the Lord's year of favour.*

Or, as Matthew begins his summary of the teaching:

> Blessed are those who feel poor in spirit!
> the realm of heaven is theirs.
> Blessed are the mourners!
> they will be consoled.
> Blessed are the humble!
> they will inherit the earth.
> Blessed are those who hunger and thirst for goodness!
> they will be satisfied.
> Blessed are the merciful!
> they will find mercy.
> Blessed are the pure in heart!
> they will see God.
> Blessed are the peacemakers!
> they will be ranked sons of God.
> Blessed are those who have been persecuted for the
> sake of goodness!
> the realm of heaven is theirs.†

Blessing, joy, freedom, peace, the Lord's year of favor!

---

* Luke 4:18-19, Moffat's translation.
† Matt. 5:3-10, Moffat's translation.

In this startling and ecstatic assurance of Jesus about the intentions of the deity we find, of course, the explanation for the outrageousness of his demands on human nature. He was well aware that these things are impossible for men. He was also aware that they are possible to God-in-men and knew that God was in fact effecting them. This was the very formula of his message, that God was beginning a new creation in man, that the "Kingdom" or "Reign" was at hand, and in fact already "among you." God was exerting his mercy in a solicitude as of the father of the Prodigal Son; God was breaking the hold of evil on the habits and impulses of men. "Behold, I saw Satan fall as lightning." God was opening to men new dimensions of love and obedience, capacities for goodness they had not before enjoyed. All Jesus' work, his teaching, his healing were directed to witness to, to demonstrate, to participate in this new attack of God on the indifference and the estrangement of men. The long awaited fulfillment of God's promised invasion of mercy, peace, and justice was now begun. When Jesus cast out "demons" it was a manifestation of the healing of the Kingdom. All those superhuman perfections set forth in the Sermon on the Mount—they, too, were manifestations of the new Reign, the new activity of God. When and where any man should be seen completely careless of self in property, reputation, family, seeking only the good of his neighbor, there, surely, was God in act, the present Kingdom. No man out of the Kingdom ever could stand so free of self-assertion.

Precisely how Jesus conceived his own vocation in this fulfillment of the Messianic dream of Judaism is not wholly clear from the gospels. The resurrection convinced his disciples and the writers of the gospels that he was precisely the *Messiah,* but evidently the disciples had not believed this during most, if not all, of their association with him. He was for most, if not all, of his career, the Messiah incognito, known to men as a prophet, a rabbi, a healer. Rembrandt, the great Protestant painter, discerned this mystery of the hidden Christ. Perhaps Jesus himself did not fully realize that he was the Messiah. But he certainly knew that the Messianic age was come, that the Law and the prophets had ceased with John, and that he himself had a unique and terrible responsibility as an agent and bearer of the inbreaking Reign of God. Yet the full implication and the precise outcome of his role were possibly not known to him. His work was to obey, and the consequences, ominous as they certainly looked at least toward the end, lay in the hands of the Father. In this case it would be first his disciples who would have the perspective of his completed work in his generation and in the history of redemption. With the key of the resurrection experiences they would discern with certainty that Jesus had been indeed *the* Messiah. And they would legitimately develop his own consciousness that he was an agent of the Kingdom to the assurance that he was the Messianic Suffering Servant who had sealed the new covenant of God's Reign by his death as well as announced it in his preaching.

A degree of human ignorance of the future is certainly apparent in Jesus' foreshortening of the fulfillment of the Reign of God. He knew of his personal experience that God had begun his new redemption, and in a sense the measure of the intensity of his sense of God's present power is to be read in his mistaken prophecies of the future. Such was the transforming might he felt about him and in him that he could not but believe that the completion of this warfare was at hand. Some of the prophecies of the imminent end of the world which are put in Jesus' mouth may have been inaccurately read back into him by the disciples and evangelists later, but his whole teaching is steeped in an ex-

pectancy and hope which might very naturally have led him
to look for the end within the lifetime of that generation,
as his disciples report him. Even so this would be a very
different view from that of the book of Revelation or of
many modern millenarians, who have slipped back into a
pre-Christian apocalypticism, losing the sense of the present
redeeming power of the Kingdom. Likewise it differs from
the other-worldly hope of "Heaven"; the God Jesus served
gave himself on this earth in the lives of men and communities, and he was to reign over such. And lastly we might
notice that this "Kingdom" was not at all to Jesus an ideal
society to be "built" by men, but was the action of God alone
in the lives of men, building true brotherhood. No man can
build that which by definition is God's building; he can
only pray for it and submit himself joyfully to it. Here is
the true dynamic of the "social gospel," for which no humanitarian idealism can substitute.

The most striking aspect of the expanding Kingdom of
God is that of "judgment," of the erection of spiritual and
moral norms before which all work-a-day human dealings
suddenly stand naked in their meanness, and men are challenged to decision with a new and terrible realization of the
urgency and finality and cosmic ramifications of their decision. The negative aspect of judgment, the fires of Gehenna,
have seemed rather strong meat to tender-hearted. Christians
of the last two centuries, but Jesus knew what he was saying.
Why is it that Jews and Christians have never taken any
interest in the notion of transmigration of souls, as we find
it in Hinduism, Buddhism, or Plato? Surely this is a neater
and more manageable speculation than the transfiguration
of each and every redeemed person. Yet there is for us,
clearly, one crucial inadequacy, its failure to take seriously
the ultimacy of the moral decisions within our historical
relationships. As heirs of an historical religion, however

little we keep of it, we all feel that we are born but once, and decide nearly every day certain issues for ever and with no recurrence.

> Once to every man and nation
> Comes the moment to decide . . .
> And the choice goes by forever
> Twixt that darkness and that light.

It was not mere traditionalism in Jesus to keep the Pharisees' visions of the Last Judgment and even hellfire in association with his faith in the fulfillment of God's Reign. There was in him a psychological and spiritual realism such as some of our greatest artists have shared. Dante knew the torments of those who refuse to choose, or choose their own hell and will not walk out the open door. Human sin swiftly hardens into psychic fetters crippling all free movement, each in its own fashion. The eyelids of the envious, in Dante, are sewn together with wire. And is not that the mark and punishment of envy, that it closes to us the vision of worth, of loveliness, of mutuality and brotherhood, and locks us in the dark poverty of our meager resources? Sexual sinners again, in Dante's vision, are tossed by a hurricane, never able to set their own course or know solid ground beneath them. What had been at first a declaration of individual liberty, a gesture of emancipation from imposed restraints, was now become itself the whip of slavery. Dostoievsky's novels, also, are full of similar characterizations of the men and women who hurry or wander over the "Nevsky promenades" of the world, the living dead, men who know neither God nor freedom but are sealed in spiritual lethargy or the psychopathic crystallizations of their own defiant evil. And so T. S. Eliot saw them in his own post-war generation, in Times Square, on Michigan Avenue, on London Bridge —"I had not thought death had undone so many!" The poets and seers have not been merely fanciful in their visions of the consequences of sin. In a situation where man must take his place and resolve his destiny in the climactic struggle against God of the powers and principalities of evil, there are consequences possible which shock the tender-minded, but which can be verified in any war or penitentiary. On this matter one is more likely to hear a realism close to that of Jesus from the Salvation Army than in the sermons attuned to the self-deceptions of our suburban congregations.

His Death and Resurrection

Even more than on the personality and teaching of Jesus, however, has the Christian fellowship dwelt on his passion and death. His last week is the only part of Jesus' lifetime which is traced with some biographical precision by the four gospels, if not with entire agreement among themselves. Paul, similarly, our earliest witness, apparently assumes the knowledge of Jesus' teaching and healing activities in his readers, but dwells again and again on his passion and resurrection. The Apostles' Creed, likewise, insists only on this in his mortal career, and down through the generations Christians have, of all the Bible, cherished most the passion story, and found their central act of worship in the dramatization of it in the Lord's Supper. What is the full significance of Jesus' suffering and execution in the fulfillment of God's purpose?

We should not overestimate the mere physical agony of crucifixion. Crucifixion is a particularly nasty and malignant way to do a man to death, but Jesus was only one such among thousands under Roman justice, and he died more mercifully than most. What of the hundreds of crosses around besieged Jerusalem in the next generation, wet with the agony of the starving who had attempted to steal through the Roman lines in the night? What of the long and horrible history of martyrs and "heretics" over the centuries, many of whom have died far more elaborately painful deaths than did Jesus himself, in his name? What of the thousands of uncomprehending women and children who were burned, starved, or bayonetted to death in the last war and its aftermath? Jesus did not occasion any remarkably shocking revelation of the perennial bestiality of man on this score.

Jesus' integrity and refusal to escape death by compromising his vocation raises him, even to the unbeliever, out of the class of uncomprehending sufferers into that of the heroic martyrs. Here his "sinlessness" is in question, and this cannot be held in any psychological sense. Jesus was full man, and tempted as we, which is to say, there was that in him which at least enjoyed a speculative toying with evil. It was no short time during which he wrestled with those perversions of his vocation which, as Dostoievsky's Grand Inquisitor has pointed out, have made their way into the very heart of some of the churches purporting to follow him. He had grown, says the Scripture record, in moral and spiritual stature, from a state of perforce lesser devotion and obedience. "Why callest thou me good," he asked at the height of his ministry, "there is none good save God." It was in heroic dedication to the work of the Kingdom that, after what had happened to John the Baptist, and many another, he set his face to Jerusalem at feast-time, to bear witness to the living God before those who recognized only the power of force or of the kept God of a hierarchy. The order of march is eloquent, Jesus walking ahead alone, the disciples huddled behind him in fear, and then the hangers-on. How late could Jesus have escaped by denying his trust? We have no means of knowing whether a retirement was still possible in that last week as he sensed the net tightening. Perhaps the night of sweaty prayer in Gethsemane armored him not merely to endure, but also to scorn to make overtures Pilate might have accepted. To the last cry, "My

God, why hast thou forsaken me?" the strain was that of a man to whom the day and hour and method of God's vindication were unknown.

The story is of the sketchiest, and we have only the most fragmentary indications of Jesus' thoughts and purposes from the time of his arrival in the city to his death. He had no confidant who perpetuated the inner history of those days, and Christians have always been driven to invest them with feelings and purposes of the personality and teaching they already knew. In itself the passion story cannot compare with the analogous account for Socrates, in Plato's *Apology, Crito,* and *Phaedo,* where the moral grandeur of the protagonist is depicted at length by one of the world's greatest writers. And yet the martyrdom of Jesus has been more fruitful than the more splendidly related martyrdom of Socrates, just in the measure that the new covenant of the living God in history is a mightier power than the most courageous dedication to truth and civic responsibility.

To define the contrast differently, the death of Socrates lies forever on the altar to justice and truth, but the living God *raised* Jesus Christ to serve on with him in his redeeming labor. The risen Christ was seen, says our earliest account, "by Cephas, then by the twelve; after that he was seen by over five hundred brothers all at once, the majority of whom survive to this day, though some have died; after that he was seen by James, then by all the apostles, and finally he was seen by myself." Of the manner of appearance of the risen Christ we have only one firsthand account, that of Paul. What confronted Paul on the Damascus road was no "natural body," of "flesh and blood," and after talking with many other witnesses of the resurrection Paul clearly stated his conviction that the risen Christ could not be of this physical character. Whatever the psychological mechanisms involved, with Paul and with the others (and Paul gives no indications that they were different in the case of the others), God used them to make apparent to these discouraged and bewildered, or even rebellious men, that the new covenant and the new promises taught and manifest in the mortal Jesus were not disrupted but even sealed by his martydom, and that Jesus Christ, the bearer of the Kingdom, lived on in power in the continuing work of the Kingdom of redemption. Here is the foundation miracle of Christianity, without which the formation of the Christian fellowship is unintelligible, just as it has been a series of confrontations with the living Christ down the generations which has perpetuated and extended the fellowship of believers. The human prophet and martyr had now "been installed as Son of God with power . . . when he was raised from the dead." Similarly Peter (in his apostolic preaching) fastened on the resurrection as the moment of adoption or transfiguration in which "God has made him both Lord and Christ, this very Jesus whom you have crucified."

As the generation which had known Jesus after the flesh passed away, the vivid knowledge of his full humanity necessarily paled and was increasingly overlaid in the mind of the Chirstian fellowship by its experiences of the risen Christ. In the teaching of Christ's work, consequently, the features of his glorified figure insensibly came to overlay the description given of his mortal life. He was increasingly described not as the Messiah incognito, but as invested in his earthly career with the powers and knowledge of himself which the disciples themselves had only discovered later. The reading back to his very birth of Jesus Christ's uniqueness was simply a utilization of a current idiom of pagan mythology to illustrate and underline the essential point that Jesus Christ was not merely a man of heroic virtue, the greatest of the prophets, but invested with a quality which set him as over a chasm from all merely good men. The very difficulty of conveying this sense of the Incarnation of God in him by a description at second hand of his

personality and sayings and doings evidently strained the
language of the evangelists. By the time of the fourth
gospel, of course, we have what might be called a devotional
commentary on the familiar story, with its strange effect of
Jesus passing through his mortal career invested already in
his resurrection glory and the foresight of after-knowledge.
Then the ground of historical reality was left entirely with
the apocryphal gnostic gospels and their denial of real suffering as revived by modern Christian Scientists. All these
idioms of an unscientific and freely symbolizing folk mind
we must learn to translate in terms of their fundamental
religious motives. Our critical scruples as to literal precision
of expression should not debar us from penetrating to the
essential truths in these pre-critical narratives.

A degree of materialization of spiritual phenomena also
took place in the tradition, much as we can observe in the
similar tradition of St. Francis. In the latter case we hear
of Francis rapt in prayer, suspended a good fifteen feet off
the ground! Similarly Clare's hearing in her cell of the
music of the Christmas service she had been hindered by ill-
ness from attending develops into the miraculous bodily
transfer to the church. The materialistic elaborations of the
resurrection story—doubting Thomas fingering the wounds,
and the various occasions on which the risen Christ consumed
food—are surely to be attributed to this natural and charming
habit of the folk mind.

Chapter VI

Protestant Principles: 2. God's Redemption and Man's Trust

∽∽

THE SECOND PRINCIPLE OF PROTESTANTISM is perhaps the most difficult to characterize. It is inextricable from what has already been said on the sufficient authority of Christ in history and from what follows on the church as the dynamic fellowship of reconcilers to that Christ. Yet no formulation of it has ever commanded such general agreement among all brands of Protestants as is the case with the evangelical conceptions of the Word and the Church. It is the evangelical understanding of the manner of man's redemption, and was usually discussed in the Reformation century in terms of Paul's and Luther's formula, "justification by faith," or the Reformed "sovereignty of God." Neither of these phrases satisfied all Protestants in the sixteenth century, and in some churches of liberal American Protestantism today they are unintelligible. Yet with all the difficulties of vocabulary and the diversities of religious temperament within Protestantism there is here a common ground of conviction and of difficulties which we may be able to suggest if not to define.

The Gift

We may begin with the sovereignty, the Kingdom, of God. This resumption of Jesus' favorite term reminds us that the Reformation was first of all no theological or organizational program, but a religious revival. Only because

men had the assurance of the presence of God himself, of
the return of Christ among them as in Dostoievsky's parable,
did they gain the courage to criticize institutions and doc-
trines long sacrosanct as the appointed ways of man's redemption. God was once again widely apprehended as the
actual present ruler of history and nature, and, in particular,
in the advance of his Kingdom in the narrower sense of the
community of those consciously dedicated to his revealed
purpose.

All these ideas were part of the universal doctrine of
Christians; what was new was the vividness and the certainty
with which they were realized. God was no longer merely
the hypothetical "first cause" and sustainer of the elaborate
system of natural processes as he had been to the "common
sense" view of Aquinas. The physical universe no longer
stood in relative independence of God, but became, as it
were, transparent and pliable as the glove upon his hand,
responsive in every part and event directly to his mysterious
will. God was no longer merely the ancient founder of the
Church, as if he had set up a trust-fund and stated executors
with discretionary powers over the distribution of his mercies.
No longer was he satisfied to permit such rationing by a legal
monopoly. God himself *acted*. He displayed himself not
merely as the goal of human idealism and contemplative
adoration, but as the Alpha, the living and free initiator and
ruler. He had not retired as the Grand Inquisitor supposed,
to leave all sovereignty to his viceregents in the hierarchy.
He would reign *directly* over the wills of men just as he
mastered directly the natural universe. Just as the institutionalism of Judaism had once crumbled before Jesus Christ's
disclosure of this God who would not be bottled up either
in Jerusalem or in Samaria and would raise up sons of
Abraham from the stones, now again his judgment and forgiveness flowed out over sacramental "validities" and pro-
prieties. The Reformation marked the shattering impact of

a new actualization of the direct Kingship of *God*. The indefinite postponement of this Kingdom which had been
the prevailing expectancy since Augustine was now consumed in a new sense of crisis, of urgency, of worlds passing
away and being rebuilt as men stood before the ultimate
realities. Before this God, man's one security and hope, as
in the days of Jesus Christ, lay in the contrite heart and
trust in his promises, in "grace alone."

It was this latter human perspective on God's sovereignty
in the process of salvation which Luther expressed in a profound reinterpretation of Saint Paul's "justification by faith."
Whoever is touched by the widening fellowship of the new
covenant knows that his acceptance into it was not earned,
that he had not made himself fit to be received by Holiness.
Those who have struggled for saintliness as did Luther and
Wesley know that not only have they fallen short, but that
human nature is incapable of saintliness by its own moral
resources or by devotion to the sacraments. Men are healed,
not by their own struggles for integrity or by mystical raptures, but by the trustful acceptance of what is done for them
by God. To be able to trust God is itself a gift of God, and
prime evidence of his redeeming activity. The man who can
trust discovers that the guilt and viciousness he knows within
himself are somehow denatured by a compassion which takes
him as he is for what he may be and makes him that. The
great cause of our human resentments and rebellion against
the universe, and our reckless fanaticisms, is simply our
inability to trust in the reconciliation which is offered to us.
We wish it rather on *our* terms, and as *our* achievement.
And the relationship of trust is the least subjective, the least
man-made of all possible bonds by which we might be linked
to the governor of our destiny. Unlike moral self-control
or mystical self-manipulation or sacramental prayer-wheels,
trust recognizes that the power to heal is found only where
there is real will to heal, in him who has in fact brought his

peace to men and does, so still. And here we arrive at the central mystery of the Christian faith, which has never been adequately formulated, of how the heroic life and death of the Lord's perfect servant brings, as it certainly does, the assurance of pardon to sinners, and reconciliation with God. Even the haziest of semi-Christians recognize the power of Jesus' example to shame us in our tepid loyalty and our bland compromises and to inspire us to better living. Jesus brings us closer to God simply by the moral influence of his integrity. But this much we also must in fairness allow to Epictetus and Socrates, and many another hero of the spirit. Christianity has always confessed an obligation of another kind to Jesus Christ. Most of the metaphors used to express it are bizarre or offensive to modern ears in one way or another, "he ransomed us from the devil," he substituted for us in advance in accepting the punishment justice requires for our sins, so that we are washed clean by "the blood of the Lamb." Some of our objections are grounded in good sense, as that to the absurd notion that God and the Devil stand in contractual relations, or that, torn between his justice and his mercy, God indulges in legal chicanery to balance his books. Yet in some way God won a unique victory over the powers of evil through the self-sacrifice of Jesus Christ. At least two elements in these views of Christ's substitution for us, moreover, point to truth, that something objective was accomplished here once for all in God's relations with man and with us, and that, whether we like it or not, vicarious suffering is part of the method of God, here and always.

Some of our objections to vicarious suffering are based on notions of justice, but most of them rest on pride. If anyone insists on suffering for me and then extending me forgiveness, this is adding insult to injury. This is the real reason why again and again I find myself trying to reject the forgiveness and reconciliation offered me in Christ.

Yet the reality and indispensability of vicarious suffering force themselves upon my observations of human relations. How many times have I been restored to balance and flexibility by some friend who stands by accepting my shame when I am in the wrong, as if to say, "Well, my friend, you have made an outrageous fool of yourself, but I believe in you." Did ever a good parent raise a child without "substituting" for him a hundred times? Is not the prodigal son perennially reestablished in dignity by his father's prodigal forgiveness of ingratitude, greed, viciousness? What good is a fine moral example to one who is already embarked obstinately on the road of sin? Sin is not merely the rejection of certain moral standards and a consequent deadening of our insight and aspiration and self-control, but it is also a wilful self-isolation. Sin always bars mutuality with some person or persons, as well as with God. The solitary cell in the prison is only the outward symbol of the criminal's inward state, and until that isolation is broken, there is no rehabilitation. To break that isolation is the work of reconciliation by vicarious suffering, to swallow distaste and shame in concern for the prisoned spirit.

That this suffering vicariously is an important element in my own experience I am reluctantly forced to admit. But must I concede this indebtedness to a Jew two thousand years ago who never dreamed of the continent on which I live? Here is the issue of the objectivity of the work and death of Jesus Christ. What was accomplished here? Surely no change in the enduring purpose of God, turning His mind from wrath to forgiveness. Rather the very death of Christ was itself an indispensable part of the disclosure of God's nature and intentions. To the disciples, convinced by the resurrection appearances that Jesus had indeed been the Suffering Servant of God, this was certainty at last that the mercy which he preached and embodied was verily the nature of God himself, whom they could now trust. To me, also, the recognition that in fact God was in Christ reconciling the world, implies that this vicarious suffering to which I acknowledge a debt, is not merely one comforting element in the battleground on which I stand, but is the most powerful factor, being indeed the work of the Kingdom Jesus witnessed to, God still reconciling the world. I am thus bound to Jesus Christ as the announcer, the initiator, the revelation of the work of the living God in pardoning and healing me. And in this way the perfect obedience, the death and resurrection of Christ, were done *for us,* even *in us.* Our mortal lives may continue shabby and unstable so that often we may search ourselves in vain for any signs of the grace to holiness, yet we still cling to the assurance that the objective and eternal and unremitting merciful holiness of God has somehow seized even us and clothed us with the promise of a righteousness beyond our powers of obedience. Our life is no longer merely our empirical all-too-human meanness, but invested in Christ and his Kingdom, in what is done for us and independently of us.

Its Reception

The Reformation insights into God's sovereignty over all created things and his initiative in the redemption of man developed into polemic theological views in two directions. There was first of all an affirmation of God's creative freedom to subdue to himself the free love of man personally with any sort of means. Such a recognition undercut all sacramentalisms and institutionalisms, which always imply limitations of the means God may normally employ. We have had occasion to observe Protestant lapses into institutionalism, Bibliolatry, sacramentalism, and other forms of *ersatz* Catholicism, but in general Protestantism has been less liable to such tendencies to idolatry and blasphemy, than to the opposite danger of seeing God in no vehicles whatever and fading out into mere secularism. God's freedom to adopt or create any means whatever, ecclesiastical or otherwise, to reconcile man to himself in Christ has remained an enduring Protestant conviction essential to evangelical Christianity.

Divine sovereignty and grace was also emphasized, by Luther and Calvin especially, at the expense of any human contribution to the process of redemption. The Reformation accounts of "justification by faith" remain as classic theological and psychological analyses of the profound spiritual crises of what William James called the "twice-born" men. This type of religious experience gave certitude and power to the great reformers, as it had to Saint Paul before them. But such an experience of God's rescue out of the depth of human frustration and failure cuts across confessional lines. Augustine knew it also and the Dominicans and Augustinians and Jansenists maintained a tradition of salvation by grace alone in the Roman Church, which forced the Council of Trent to straddle the issue while repudiating Lutheran language. Within Protestantism, on the other hand, the humanist and Anabaptist wings did not generally understand the Lutheran and Calvinist depreciation of man's contribution to his own salvation. They recognized the initiative of God in the process, so far as they were evangelicals at all, but they cannot be classified under the Pauline pattern any more than the whole New Testament witness can be reduced to this type. The Quakers felt more affinity to the mystical Johannine view, while many of the Anabaptists and humanists dropped most readily into the moralistic Jewish categories of the first three gospels. It was not usually a matter of denying the Pauline "justification by faith" so much as a less self-conscious and analytical experience of commitment of the heart and will to God.

With the fading of the vision of the first Reformers, moreover, the general Protestant understanding of salvation went through much the same evolution which occurred in the generations immediately following Paul. Justification by faith was enshrined centrally in the confessions of the chief evangelical churches, but there is no institutional way of preserving the religious insight itself. "Faith" came increasingly to revert to its "Catholic" meaning of "assent to propositions" in place of trust in a personal God, and "justification by faith" was then a justification which could be earned by human effort—precisely what Paul and Luther had intended to preclude by the phrase in the first place. Luther had returned again and again to the fundamental contrast between the two types of faith:

> There are two kinds of believing: first a believing about God which means that I believe that what is said of God is true. This faith is rather a form of knowledge than a faith. . . . Men possessing it can say, repeating what others have said: I believe that there is a God. I believe that Christ was born, died, rose again for me. But what the real faith is, and how powerful a thing it is, of this they know nothing . . . they think that faith is a thing which they may have or not have at will, like any other natural human thing; so when they arrive at a conclusion and say "Truly the doctrine is correct, and therefore, I believe it," then they think that this is faith.
>
> When faith is of the kind that *God* awakens and creates in the heart, then a man trusts in Christ. He is then so securely founded on Christ that he can hurl defiance at sin, death, hell, the devil and all God's enemies. He fears no ill, however hard and cruel it may prove to be . . . such faith which throws itself upon God, whether in life or in death, alone makes a Christian man. . . . It kills the past and reconstitutes us utterly different men in heart, disposition, spirit and in all the faculties. . . . Oh! there is something vital, busy, active, powerful about this faith that simply makes it impossible ever to let up in doing good works. The believer does not stop to ask whether good works are to be done, but is up and at it before the question is put. . . . Faith is a lively, reckless confidence in the grace of God . . . so it is that a man unforced acquires the will and feels the impulse to do good to everybody, serve everybody and suffer everything for the love and praise of

God who has bestowed such grace upon him. . . . Pray to God that he work this faith in you: otherwise you will never, never come by it, feign all that you will, or work all you can.*

Despite such warnings, Lutherans and Calvinists worked all they could and feigned all they would as if faith were a thing they might have or have not at will, and were able to deny the very meaning of justification by faith while insisting with fanaticism on its words. Thus was the ground laid for the triumph of rationalism and moralism in the eighteenth century. Modern Protestantism has known nearly as many attempts as modern Romanism to supplement or replace the Reformation justification by faith with descriptions taking their departure from human freedom and responsibility. Religious revivals within Protestantism, to be sure, seem usually to return to the Pauline view, but it would not be accurate to call this the universally accepted Protestant interpretation of the way of salvation either in the twentieth or the sixteenth century. In both centuries, however, this has probably been the dominant Protestant interpretation. "Catholicism," on the other hand, has never been able to repudiate it fully. In the first decades of the Reformation, negotiators who hoped to heal over the split found this one of the areas most amenable to adjustment. And in our own day, at the Edinburgh Conference in 1937, Protestants, Orthodox, and Anglo-Catholics were happy to discover that they could phrase a mutually satisfactory statement on God's grace and man's free response in the process of salvation. Perhaps it would be fair to state that with regard to the manner of man's reconciliation, Protestants agree that God is the initiator and aggressive agent, with a sovereign and unlimited choice of means at his disposal, but are not entirely agreed as to precisely how much or what kind of freedom man exercises in his response to God.

---

* Lindsay, T. M., *History of the Reformation,* I, 429, 430, 431, 445. (Chas. Scribner's Sons, New York, 1912).

Chapter VII

Protestant Principles: 3. The Protestant Conception of the Church

~~~~~~

FROM THE GOOD NEWS of new health for humanity we may turn to the community which actualizes this message, and a third Protestant conception, the frequently misunderstood "priesthood of all believers." This conception constitutes still an unsurmountable hurdle for all efforts toward unity with Orthodox or with Roman Catholics.

Evangelical Fellowship

Protestants as well as their opponents have often represented this principle to mean simply the religious emancipation of the individual, as if to say, "every man his own priest." That emphasis on the inescapable responsibility of every individual to come to terms with God personally is indeed intended here, but this is not the primary weight of the principle. The wider meaning is rather "every man his neighbor's priest," or, to drop the term "priest," "the mutual ministry of all believers." The formula is thus in reality equivalent to Luther's favorite description of the church, "the communion of saints," meaning by "saints" not men who had achieved moral perfection, but those who were saved by trust, "believers." "Mutual ministry," however, expresses more emphatically than "communion," the dynamic character of the Christian fellowship.

The blessings of Christian fellowship are not once received and then passively enjoyed. The primary function of that fellowship is to transmit God's reconciling love in the lives and words of its members, and so long as the fellowship remains in Christ, that process is continuous. We may bring in here still a third emphasis much used by the Reformers. There is a true portion of the church of Christ, they said, wherever the message of redemption in Christ is truly presented in preaching, in the sacraments, or in men's lives and *where it is received*. The ministering thus must be effective, must kindle like fire and evoke kindred response before we are sure God is in the work. The highly corporate emphasis of all these terms shows the Reformation protest against the individualism of late medieval Catholicism. Evangelical Protestantism means "social religion," as John Wesley was to say later, it means communion, mutual ministry, the sharing of the most sacred things in life, it means the Body of Christ, the Church. Calvin thus takes up the saying of the early church, "No man can have God for his father who has not the Church for his mother." And Luther likewise directed "anyone who is to find Christ must first find the Church." He is not to "trust to himself, nor by the help of his own reason build a bridge of his own to heaven" but to unite with the people who believe in Christ. Outside the actual fellowship of those who live to Christ, the living Christ is not to be discovered. And within this fellowship of believers the first Protestant virtue is mutuality, in contrast to the primary Romanist virtue, submission.

This true church, evangelical and catholic, is not defined by institutional limits. Protestantism recognizes all as Christians who sincerely respond in faith to the tender of Christ in the gospel and sacraments, however perverted be their church administration or theology. And this insight is found among the least educated. An evangelical peasant woman was once accosted during the "missionary" campaign of the storm troopers of Louis XIV of France. The devout and humane priest Fénelon asked her, "Where was your faith before Luther?" "In the hearts of people like you," she

answered. What theologian could have done better? There
is no certainty that the true Church will ever be purely and
exclusively manifest in any institution, Protestant, Roman
Catholic or Orthodox.

The fellowship of Christians can be defined as the community of the forgiven and forgiving. They are a company
exclusively of sinners, but their rebellion and estrangement
from God and each other and from their own consciences
has been overcome. Only as overcome, in fact, are Christians able to face themselves in their full stature as sinners,
for without a presentiment of a pardon our instinct of moral
self-preservation would not permit this confession. No one
ever explores so much of hell as the saints, for they alone
dare to lay bare in themselves levels of self-assertion and
malignancy whose very existence the merely respectable man
would deny. The redeemed can afford to admit guilt and
thereby to burst the psychic bonds of evil. They can even
assume the shame of others, binding themselves to the guilt
of men about them with whom they live in natural associations. God sets this community of thieves to catch more
thieves.

In every nation and continent there are cells of this hidden fifth column, this leaven in which the community building powers of the Kingdom are at work, and where also is
hardened the courage to say "No!" when necessary, to the
demands of nation, race, or class. Taking up into their own
hearts the terrible tensions of our age, accepting the weight
of oppression and exploitation, or perhaps the retribution
long due their nation or race or class, and by their bruises,
healing—such are the faithful. We do not know who they
are, save as we hear of a handful here and a couple there,
but we know they are there and everywhere as the chosen
of God unto whom the spirit of Christ Jesus is close. In
our day, especially, their labors of pity and mercy are often
but half-consciously "in the name of Christ." They are the

quickest discovered under persecution, when their quiet endurance singles them out from the bitter and violent and weak. In the success of good causes, on the other hand, they are usually unidentified among the fair-weather virtuous and those who make a living jumping on bandwagons. Unto them alone is committed the "power of the keys" of heaven and hell, for by their testimony to justice and mercy they condemn the wicked, and by their forgiveness they heal the repentant and bring them to eternal life. In the irrevocable decisions for or against the Kingdom are men thus bound or loosed to eternity.

We have been speaking not of the churches, but of the Church, those in whom the spirit of the Messiah, the Suffering Servant, dwells and labors at his reconciliation today. This is the true Christian fellowship, created by a call and nourished by the living word, in which all are members one of another and the head is Christ. To apply this description to any church congregation or institution in America or elsewhere would provoke a smile, and indeed it should. The churches manifest extremely little of Christ's passionate reconciling aggressiveness. As institutions many of them seem to be rather associations of idealists, dedicated to the "ethics of Jesus," or organizations for the perpetuation of this or that creedal statement or liturgical practice or form of government. No such institution should be taken for the Church, yet most of them in their pathetic ways bear witness to the Kingdom down the generations, the memory of its beginning, the disturbing sense of its hidden presence, the hope of its perfection into which the churches may dissolve. And for this interim the churches with all their tepidity and unfaithfulness are necessary. They represent the culture, so to speak, of the Holy Spirit, and preserve an infinitely precious tradition. One needs to steep himself in that culture, its Bible, its hymns, its liturgy and prayer, its music and art, its creeds and theology, to learn the full rich-

ness of God's revelation. And yet to serve the true Church
and its Lord, we must also be merciless on the churches, that
is, on ourselves.

Christian Institutions

Let us then review the several agencies and aspects of the
institutional churches from this Protestant understanding
of the true Church. The ministry, the preaching of the
Word, the sacraments, the government of the church may
all be touched on here. The Bible as a means of grace will
be treated in the next chapter.

The principle of the mutual ministry of believers has implications, first of all, for the status and functions of the
Protestant clergy. The Protestant clergyman can never claim
the distinct spiritual status and the peculiar prerogatives of
a priest in the Orthodox or Roman Catholic sense. On all
fundamental matters he is only another "believer," of the
same rank with the "ministers" in the pews. Not all men
and women in the Christian fellowship have the qualities
of mind and body to conduct public worship effectively, to
preach, to interpret the Scriptures profitably at some length,
to conduct sacraments with dignity and beauty. Some of
these functions also require special training. The evangelical
clergyman, however, performs them all only in a representative capacity for the fellowship; he is articulating the
life animating all. The ministrations of the clergyman, in
fact, may not be the most effective expression of the reconciling power in the community. By the visible integrity of
their lives, housewives may often minister Christ more effectively to each other than can a clergyman whose house-
keeping experience is desultory. As Luther has it, all believing laymen "are worthy to appear before God, to pray
for others, to teach each other mutually the things that are
of God . . . so ought we freely to help our neighbors by
our body and our works, and each should become to the

other a sort of Christ, so that we may be mutually Christs, and that the same Christ may be in all of us." The Quakers make the point clear by exaggerating it. They have no permanent ministry (in their classical type); the message of the Word is spoken in their meetings by whoever feels a vocation to the public ministry on that particular occasion.

At the other extreme from the Friends, the Anglicans, Presbyterians and Reformed, and some Lutherans maintain an exalted conception of the role of the regular evangelical ministry. While all believers are truly and equally ministers of Christ, the regular clergy perform highly significant functions. They are, for example, by far the strongest force for continuity in the Christian fellowship down the generations. They are equipped by special training to reinterpret the experience and tradition of the fathers both as guide and corrective to the passing moods and enthusiasms of the rising generations, in theology or worship or ethics. Through the trained clergy the local congregations have what is normally their sole avenue to the aspirations and failures, the holiness and struggles of generations of Christians who lived by faith and were not to be perfected apart from us. To the local congregation, again, it is the regular minister who in overwhelming degree represents the larger church of the present generation. He has been ordained, as a rule, at the hands of other clergy. Through him come the relations with administrative bodies for the common enterprises of local congregations, missions, religious education, philanthropies and the like. Whether he intends it or not, the minister represents in his person the whole Church, living and dead, to his congregation, and in particular the actively evangelistic apostolate of the believing community, reaching back in unbroken continuity to the disciples. His own character and spiritual gifts and insights are highly important, yet he never speaks from them alone.

By thus representing the whole church, finally, the regular

clergy constitute the focus of Christian independence of cultural movements, nationalistic, political, social. Just as the regular clergy of the primitive church crystallized partly out of the need of the Christian movement to consolidate against cultural perversions and political persecution of the faith, so the analogous pressures in our day are leading Protestants to recast their thinking on the nature of the ministry. The historic episcopate of the Anglicans or the succession of ordaining presbyters among the Reformed, together with their administrative functions, need to be measured anew by the jealously laic wing of Baptists, Disciples and Congregationalists who have perhaps oversimplified the priesthood of all believers.

When Protestant ministers claim any unique religious status, however, as they have done now and again, then they have left evangelical grounds to become priests again, "new presbyter but old priest writ large." Recognizing the long-run importance of the regular ministry, Protestantism has normally taken particular pains to make sure that the public and stated minister of the fellowship of mutual ministers is a *believer*. All the Reformed churches require that their clergy undertake such functions only in their own conviction that they are impelled by the Spirit to do so, and only in the consent of the congregation to their services. The "Catholic" priest, by contrast, is usually put to priestly training before he is old enough to have any sense of vocation. He is not expected to voice the continuous ministry of the fellowship; he is expected merely to perform the sacraments. For that he needs neither a vocation in the Protestant sense, nor the consent of his parishioners. The sacraments, as objects in themselves and apart from the fellowship, are his authority and prerogative.

The "mutual ministry of all believers," of course, undercuts also this priestly monopoly of the means of God's mercy. The Anglo-Catholic, Orthodox, and Roman sacraments are "valid" only when performed under certain rigid conditions and by certain qualified priests. Were these churches to admit the priesthood of all, they must then concede that the sacraments only mediate, if in heightened vividness and concentration, the same reconciliation of God mutually ministered within the fellowship, and that thus they are not absolutely indispensable. This they cannot admit. The apostolic and evangelical sacraments are vehicles of the free personal love of God, but the Catholic views the grace received as an impersonal *thing*, like a blood transfusion whose virtue is independent of the personal relations of donor and recipient. The only indispensable sacraments in the Protestant conception are those available to all believers in the testimony of their words and lives. The ecclesiastical sacraments are solemn, dramatic, and corporate manifestations of the *same mercies*. What is offered in the preaching of the Word is Christ. What is offered in the living of the Word is Christ. What is offered in the Lord's Supper is Christ. With the exception of the high liturgy of silence, the Quakers have an ultra-puritanical distaste for ceremonies, yet they know a baptism and a communion "of the Spirit" in their close-knit fellowship. While most Protestants would feel that highly useful and normally harmless aids to the articulation and freshening of faith are here rejected, yet if the Friends minister the Word successfully in the spirit alone, they have done what was necessary in the Protestant view of ministry and sacraments.

The Reformation forms of the sacraments in several ways recovered the relevance to Christian fellowship which the priestly monopoly had lost. Prayers and Scripture were in a language everyone could understand and there could be genuine participation by the laity. All were expected to partake often of Holy Communion, and in the Reformed church the practice was adopted of circulating the elements through the congregation in token of the mutual ministry of believers, rather than having all repair to the officiating clergy at the rail. And perhaps most important of all was the recovery of the congregational singing of the ancient church. The prescribed Gregorian chant, denied to the laity, was now replaced by free congregational participation. The austere beauty of the Genevan psalms with Bourgeois' music, and the rich flowering of Lutheran hymnody mark the recovery of a corporate spirit and a new richness in worship, despite the elimination of saints and censers.

As to the organization and government of the institutional church, the priesthood of all means the participation of all believers in government. With modern Rome "the church," practically speaking, means the clergy (if not the pope, on the principle, *l'église c'est moi*). The laity are purely passive in administration as in teaching. But where all believers are "priests," the government of the church cannot be absolutist, but must be representative from the local congregation to the whole church catholic. As we have seen, the ancient church and Eastern Orthodoxy held on the whole, to this pattern of government, and the whole Western church adopted it in the early years of the fifteenth century at the time of the councils. When the monarchical papacy recaptured the machinery of church government, the conciliar tradition of representative democracy was forced into Protestantism. This is the significance of the Reformation in constitutional history. All the Reformers appealed to a free general assembly of the church to arbitrate on the issues of the Reformation, but the papacy knew better than to permit such an assembly. When the Council of Trent was finally summoned, it had been carefully rigged and was expertly steered. Rome has feared nothing more than a free general council since the middle of the fifteenth century, even if its attendance is to be limited to Romanists.

On Protestant soil, however, the representative principle

was consistently applied to local units and up to the largest units feasible. Only the Calvinist churches were able to carry through this pattern on a national and occasionally international scale. The separatists desired no government beyond that of the independent congregations, and the Lutherans and Anglicans were inhibited by political interference. Luther's original intentions for the German evangelicals were apparently equivalent to the pattern later worked out by the Calvinists, but the disorder of the class wars of the first decade of the Reformation convinced him that responsible and stable Christians were too rare in the congregations to risk it. Thus the use of evangelical princes as "emergency bishops" in the Lutheran churches became permanent and both congregational and synodical life was precluded until Lutheranism in America should one day have freedom to develop on principles congenial to the mutual ministry of all believers. The Anglicans, likewise, found their church organization captured by the monarchy, and both national and diocesan assemblies were prohibited altogether for generations. Even in our own day the control of Anglican affairs by a parliament including dissenters, atheists, and Jews, and the appointment of governing bishops by non-Anglican prime ministers have raised grave questions.

The Protestant principle of representative government is not to be understood as a replacing of the divine right of the pope by a divine right of the people, or of the majority. Representative government can make mistakes; it is not infallible. But just because it recognizes its fallibility, it provides means for retrieving its errors. All Protestant assemblies of dignitaries may err, and sometimes do. Recognizing this possibility, they do not make the irrecoverable and appalling errors of the "infallible" papacy, nor with the Orthodox, bind all generations absolutely to the theological vocabulary of the fourth and fifth centuries.

Chapter VIII

Protestant Principles: 4. The Bible

∞∞∞

How Not to Read It

TO MANY IT IS ODD or even offensive that the crucial knowledge of God should be found in a book, printed by this or that firm, sold over the counter, read to tatters or left on a parlor table to petrify. God should use more dignified means, and much less particular ones, at least sermons in stones and running brooks if not the pillars of cloud and fire. He should have inscribed his purposes in the consciences of all men, or at least all the philosophers, or made them apparent in the unchanging majesties of nature. A book is so much subject to circumstance, so outrageously unique and specific a channel for universal truth!

The fact that the true understanding of God should be found in a mere book, however, is a necessary consequence if God has revealed himself in history, since a history must be recorded. And this is the chief ground of offense. Most of the world's higher religions and nearly all of the world's classical philosophies proceed on the contrary assumption, that the nature of ultimate reality and of man's adjustment to it are unaffected by the transitory and unsystematic ebb and flow of history. Man finds God perhaps by ceasing to concern himself with historical activity, by rising in contemplative abstraction to the unchanging absolutes, accounting the world of events *Maya* or illusion. Or, if more actively inclined, he finds principles of decision in eternal and universal moral laws of conscience as with Kant and the Stoics. There is something arbitrary in the contention of the historical religions that God himself is concerned with that conflict of wills and community purposes which make history, and that certain human purposes are more directly related to *his* purposes than those of other communities. As the old line runs:

> How odd
> that God
> should choose
> the Jews.

Human history, however, is generally arbitrary and "undemocratic" in these matters. No one who knows anything about it supposes that the English-speaking drama has ever again reached the heights it knew in the days of Queen Elizabeth, or that automobile manufacture anywhere has ever equalled contemporary Detroit, or that any Western people save possibly Germany has ever contributed so much to philosophy as did Athens. Nine-tenths of those who assert that all the higher religions teach the same truths are only voicing their prejudice against the actual variety and inequality of human history, and have not, in fact, studied the character of any of the higher religions. Anyone who has ever been touched by prophetic religion and wishes to learn the ways of God with human communities, will read the history of the Hindus and Greeks and Egyptians and Chinese with dissatisfaction and meager profit, and even despite himself return to the Jews and that greatest of Jews in the world's unique sourcebook of the redemption of history, the Bible.

And yet the Bible is a difficult book for the modern educated man to read. Our very training in critical scientific thinking has strangely handicapped us in our attempts to interpret the idiom of imaginative writing of the pre-scientific age. The habit of scientific thought, precise, colorless, literal, gives us great powers of manipulating our environment, but it inhibits our understanding and our own deepest self-expression. We cannot handle symbolism and imagery confidently. We would like to believe that everything of meaning in religious symbols can be stated boldly in propositions to which one may say "Yes" or "No." At least this is what has been very widely done to the Bible in the last three hundred years, both by those who have said "Yes" and by those who have said "No." Thus great numbers have taken it as literally and crassly meant that God walked in the garden and the serpent spoke with an audible voice and that Joshua stalled the whirling cosmos and Jonah, like Pinocchio, survived the digestive fluids of the whale, and have supposed, furthermore, that one must believe all this and more or be no Christian. The literal and precise temper of modern science has thus conquered the very people who supposed they were defending the faith against science. They were betrayed by an overly rationalistic and utilitarian education into a fundamental misunderstanding of what they held most sacred, defending what was untenable and worthless and often losing what was most true and important.

A wooden and literal interpretation of the Bible, however, is often no worse than an allegorical exegesis which seeks the same goal of reducing the whole literature to theological and scientific propositions. According to the procedure advocated by Thomas Aquinas, for example, every passage of Scripture bears three types of allegorical sense besides its straightforward literal meaning. By means of these several types of allegory, a variety of doctrinal and moral theses can be extracted from any passage by the exercise of moderate ingenuity. When the literal meaning seems to conflict with what the present pope enjoins, then the interpreter must understand an orthodox allegorical sense to be the true meaning of the passage. By this type of interpretation the fundamental historical character of the Bible can be lost altogether in the intoxicating exercise of uncontrolled allegorizing. If a mischievous demon were to convert the pope to Islam or Buddhism, some loyal Jesuit would surely extract either system from the Scriptures in good faith on Thomist principles. Books can be written, to be sure, with all four levels of meaning, as Dante proved in his *Divine Comedy*. But with the exception of a few books like the Gospel of John, or Revelation, the Bible was *not* written on four levels, or in allegorical style. The simple historical meaning is the intended meaning in the great majority of cases, and the Reformation reading of it so in the believing community brought to light the unity and coherence of the Bible as the makers of the canon saw it. There is no absolute certainty about even literal meanings, of course, in some few passages, and the authoritative theological doctrine of the Scriptures is not always unambiguous in the Protestant reading. Those things can only be absolutely and finally ascertained by Roman Catholic methods of reading them in where they are not, and if one prefers those things to the living Word, he can dispense with the Bible altogether.

For an instance of Romanist interpretation of the Bible we may return to the question of the freedom of the Virgin Mary from original sin. The findings of reputable scholarship on this subject are briefly indicated in the *Encyclopaedia Britannica*. The character of Romanist interpretation, by contrast, may be illustrated by the monument erected before the Palace of the Propaganda in Rome on the occasion of the definition of the Immaculate Conception. The marble statue of the Virgin is flanked by four figures who "prophesied" of her freedom from original sin: Moses, David, Isaiah and Ezekiel. Apart from the fact that two of the figures thus immortalized did not write the prophecies they are credited with, to read into the passages concerned any mention of Mary would be a *tour de force*, to say nothing of her "immaculate conception." The clearest prophecy comes from "Moses," and is found in that curse of God on the serpent in the Garden of Eden, "I will set a feud between you and the woman, between your brood and hers; they shall strike at your head, and you shall strike at their heel." The word for "brood," masculine in the Hebrew, became feminine in the Latin translation and was enough to indicate to Roman scholars that "she" who would grind the head of Satan without being touched herself by sin could be none other than Mary *immaculate*. No one who is unable to follow the cogency of this argument should undertake to understand the vast tissue of such interpretations which constitutes Roman Biblical scholarship.

The stability of this scholarship was insured early in this century by the institution of a Papal Biblical Commission. The voting members of this commission were selected from prelates free from such prejudices as they might have acquired by any training in historical study of Biblical literature and gifted with what scholarly judgment is refined in long years of administrative experience. It was this commission which, amid other strange and wonderful findings, decided for the Romanist obedience that Moses wrote the bulk of the first five books of the Bible, that Isaiah wrote the prophecies numbered from chapter forty on in the book of Isaiah, that Matthew is the earliest of the gospels, and that all three of the synoptic gospels were written before 70 A.D., that it is historically certain that the Gospel of John was written by John the son of Zebedee and that it narrates the actual speeches of Jesus, that not even the Apostles, to say nothing of Jesus, believed that the second coming and the triumph of the Kingdom was imminent. The absolute inerrancy of the Scriptures, even in matters irrelevant to faith or morals, is insisted on with all the forces of the most ignorant and obscurantist Protestant fundamentalist. The entertaining but saddening caricature of scholarly argument by which Roman Biblical interpreters regularly proceed from a show of historical knowledge and method to predetermined orthodox conclusions such as these can be readily recognized by those who have seen the degradation of scholarship to propaganda in Nazism and Bolshevism. No totalitarianism, even the most humanitarian, can tolerate the free search for historical truth.

The fundamental error in this method of Biblical interpretation is the attempt to deduce from the Bible a comprehensive and closed system of philosophical and dogmatic truths, instead of letting the Bible speak in its own terms. Any such static syllabus will possess elements which will conflict with other knowledge in the progress of science and will become simply incredible. In the literalist or Romanist conception they must nevertheless be affirmed by Christians by some "sacrifice of the intellect." But Christianity is not a philosophy, although it has prompted many philosophies. Much less is it an astronomy or geology. It does not matter to Christianity whether the earth was created in six days or six billion, whether it rests on pillars with water above the sky, or whether this fellow Copernicus is right after all. A believing Christian can well afford to be agnostic over very extensive ranges of subjects, including even such as the reasons for suffering and sin, for the inequalities of human destiny, spiritual as well as physical, the nature of life after death, hell-fire, the fate and meaning of the unredeemed and of the vicious, angels, demons, many types of alleged miracles. Our own experience of growing insight should warn us against hasty dogmatic rejections, and we should always hold our minds open on elements which are, or have been, significant to others in the Christian fellowship. The great central affirmations, however, are those by which men live, and if we have adequate direction for our living in this confusing world, we do not need to have it all explained. Christianity does not pretend to explain it; Christianity is not a "system," it is a commitment, a community of faith.

The History of Redemption

If we are able to free ourselves of this habit of treating
the Bible as a manual of science, philosophy and ethics we
will be on the way to an understanding of the principle on
which it was assembled, and for which it should be read.
Unlike Greek or Hindu myths, which illustrate eternal truths,
the Biblical accounts trace specific and unique dealings with
men of the living God. And as befits the living God, the
dominant literary structure of the Bible and of the Christian
self-consciousness in general is not philosophical meditation or ethical discourse, but narration, the account of what
God has *done* at certain times and places. Even genealogies
and priestly enthusiasms about liturgical equipment have
their place in the Bible in so far as they contribute to an
understanding of the meeting of God's will and man's, of
that series of rebellions, reconciliations, promises, punishments which the Bible contains. God acts in all history, of
course, but it is in this particular history that his presence
and purpose in the face of human indifference, defiance and
obedience are uniquely exposed because of the unique awareness of this people, or some among them. All men see the
unending rise and decline of the peoples of this world, and
many hold it meaningless. It is as if the writers of Scripture
viewed the crumbling cities through glasses polarized to
reveal the devouring flame of divine judgment invisible to
the naked eye. With such an insight of the living God at
work, the relation of this particular people to him was lifted
to a new dimension of consciousness both in its reverence
and in its apostasy. Those who have glimpsed Jehovah
trampling the winepress, or gathering his sheep as a shepherd
can never make their day-to-day decisions in the innocence
of earlier days.

We can recover some sense of how the Bible was written
and how it was read in a pre-scientific Christianity by listen-

ing to preaching like that of *Green Pastures*. Much preaching in quasi-illiterate communities is a dramatic expansion on the Bible stories, into which the congregation enters even audibly, done with considerable freedom and no literalistic inhibitions. The book itself is no infallible and untouchable record. Rather the Bible drops away as a prompting script and its characters are felt as real and living persons—Joshua, Moses, Jesus, Paul. Their histories are told over with all sorts of variations and even humor within the believing congregation. God himself is realized as a present "person" and can be treated with startling familiarity ("Have a ten-cent seegar, Lord?") even while the weight of his judgment is brought home, and the wonder of his forgiveness. The whole interpretation is in many ways similar to some of the more reverent medieval mystery plays. The congregation has a tact for the religious essence of the story, and is quite careless about literal exactitude in details. While no doubt is felt about the historical truth of the account, critical standards of precise and verified history are not understood or applied. This is the type of group tradition of which most of our Bible is the written record, and for the reenactment of which the Bible has served down through many centuries in the Christian fellowship. We moderns are baffled by it because we have almost entirely lost the practice of congregational revivification whereby the Bible becomes again a prompter's script for the dialogue of man and God. We can neither dismiss the Bible as wholly legendary nor, on the other hand, rest confident in it as scientifically true when we regard it primarily as a body of information and propositions. Truly we must become again as little children (through whatever process of sophistication) before we can enter the Kingdom of religious and artistic communication and understanding.

Our evangelical understanding of the nature of the Church, however, prepares us for the reception of the disclosure of God through the Scriptures. We are from the beginning free from the dead hand of a tradition or an authority claiming finality. All branches of Christendom have always held the Bible to be in some sense authoritative, and all branches ancient and modern, except Romanism, have always urged lay reading of the Bible. Different answers, and different kinds of answers, however, have been given to the question, "Who is to interpret the Scriptures?" "Only the hierarchy with the pope," says Rome, "and in the light of the fathers so far as they can be represented as being in accord with the reigning pope." And while Eastern Orthodoxy encourages far greater latitude in popular devotions, on major controversies her churches too would reply "Only by the hierarchy so far as it agrees with the consensus of the fathers." What of Protestantism? Here the "mutual ministry of believers" implies an answer of a different type. There is no institutionally located static authority. Like the church itself, authoritative interpretation is a dynamic process. The Scriptures are interpreted out of the shared experience of the believing community, the Holy Spirit witnessing in each and in each to each other of the truth of what is intended *for us*. By means of the scholarship of the learned men in the fellowship, the views of the fathers are also contributed to the conversation, on the principle, as T. S. Eliot puts it, of "giving the dead a vote," but not as infallible opinions. Every individual believer is both expositor and learner of the message of salvation, and while some are always granted more weight at any given time than others, none are infallible and none are to be dismissed without a hearing.

The Reformation marked a tremendous flowering of group study of the Bible. Nearly every Protestant hearth became the seat of a permanent seminar on the significance of the daily family readings and the varieties of prayer meetings and reading circles have been endless. The only secure position with regard to the Word is joyful humble participation in the common effort of the Christian fellowship to search and to obey. Time and again this Protestant method of seeking the will of God for his people has led to disagreement. So long as the disagreement is contributed in humility to the mutual ministrations of the Word within the enduring fellowship that is as it should be. As soon as any one formulation is removed from discussion and set up as final, then evangelical Protestantism has been abandoned for a substitute institutionalism. As the Scots Confession puts it quaintly of its interpretation of the Word of God:

> Protestand that gif onie man will note in this our confessioun onie artickle or sentence repugnand to Gods halie word, that it wald pleis him of his gentleness and for christian charities sake to admonish us of the same in writing; and we upon our honoures and fidelitie, be Gods grace do promise unto him satisfactioun fra the mouth of God, that is fra his halie scriptures, or else reformation of that quilk he sal prove to be amisse.

No person public nor private, nor any church can claim of itself the prerogative of final determination of God's Word. It may not be easy to persuade a Scotsman, but as a true Protestant he can never deny you a trial. All Protestant creedal formulations and theologies, so long as they are Protestant, must be tentative in this sense, always standing under correction of the continuing preaching and hearing of the Word in Scripture in the evangelical church catholic.

The Bible does not argue, but assumes, the interaction with human purposes of a purpose more tenacious, more patient than the sense of destiny of any people or civilization. The possibility of such an interaction is precisely what we should like to argue, yet the Bible haunts us. However deeply we bury the awareness in our subconscious minds, we know that we are seen, and judged, and we know it because the writers of the Bible knew it first. Ideas about God we can juggle more or less expertly, but the unpredictable, the actual, the living God is the skeleton that will not rest silently in the closet. At the moment, perhaps, the Bible is too little read or preached and consequently the will and activity of God in our immediate crises are most imperfectly discerned. Presently, however, as so often before, the Bible will again be waited on in the listening congregation as the prompting script of God's dialogue with *this* generation, and presently God's intention will be known and obeyed.

Chapter IX

Protestant Principles:
5. Ethics and Politics

∞∞

The Protestant "Vocation"

WE HAVE COMMENTED on the ultimate source and authority of evangelical faith, the evangelical conception of the way of salvation, and the nature of the evangelical church and Bible. We may now consider certain characteristically Protestant views of Christian life and conduct.

For a first generalization, it may be said that Protestantism rejected the double standard in Christian ethics which had been prevalent since Constantine, and once again laid on the consciences of all Christians the full gospel requirement of perfection.

Evangelical perfection, it will be recalled, was, from the days of Constantine, the aspiration only of the monk. The monkish life was consequently referred to as "the religious" life, and the word "vocation," or "calling," was restricted to this way of life, which of all ways of life was particularly called and dedicated to God. All other activities of society were, from the religious point of view, just ways of earning a living. Down through the history of monasticism, however, many of these activities had been integrated into the religious "vocation" of the monk. He had come to intersperse his prayers with a variety of types of labor, farming, fishing, sheep-raising, wine-making, carpentry, stenographic and editorial work, school teaching, scholarship and systematic thought—and all regarded as *ad gloriam dei,* forms of enacted prayer. As Brother Lawrence was to say later, he could be as sensible of the presence of God amid all the bustle and flurry and pots and pans of a busy kitchen, as he could on his knees before the sacrament. Now came Brother Martin, who had been an exemplary monk for decades, to say that all these values of the monastic life were available to any believer who would go about his regular legitimate business with the dedication and religious spirit of monasticism at its best. Every legitimate activity could become a "vocation" if undertaken as a means of serving God, and as we have previously observed, could become a highly effective form of "preaching" the gospel to others engaged in the same activity. Thus at the same time that "Protestant" princes were closing down and confiscating monastic establishments everywhere in a shameless campaign of loot, Protestantism turned the spirit of monastic discipline loose in the world and could have said with even more truth than Francis of Assisi, "the world is our cloister."

This spirit of monastic discipline so poured out into the varied activities of modern civilization is nobly stated in Calvin's *Institutes of the Christian Religion:*

> We are not our own; therefore neither our reason nor our will should predominate in our deliberations and actions.
>
> We are not our own; therefore let us not presuppose it as our end to seek what may be expedient for us according to the flesh.
>
> We are not our own; therefore let us, so far as possible, forget ourselves and all things that are ours.
>
> On the contrary, we are God's; to him, therefore, let us live and die.
>
> We are God's; therefore let his wisdom and will preside in all our actions.
>
> We are God's; towards him, therefore, as our only legitimate end, let every part of our lives be directed. (Bk. III, ch. 7, 1.)

These Protestant "vocations in the world" became the means of the greatest penetration of Christianity into culture which the history of the faith has seen. As we have noticed before, this was to be a regulation of political and economic and social and cultural life, no longer by the occasional external intervention of the clerical hierarchy, but from *within,* by the dedicated consciences of Protestant monks-in-the-world. This was the work primarily of the Calvinist-influenced churches of France, Switzerland, Holland, England, Scotland, and New England, and while it lasted at full strength only about three generations, to the middle or end of the seventeenth century, its impact on the enduring life and institutions of all these countries has been immeasurable. We are still living in the backwash of this mightiest attempt of Christianity to make the kingdoms of this world confess the Kingdom of God, and while the forms of this Calvinist and Puritan discipline are not much more applicable than the medieval pattern Rome is still recommending for the present crisis in Western civilization, nevertheless the memory of these attempts should give us courage and guidance.

The conception of a Christian vocation was conceived in Lutheranism in too passive a sense to be widely effective in transforming society. Luther was socially conservative and thought still in terms of agrarian society with its class divisions of peasants and landlords. A vocation for him was largely a matter of accepting one's appointed station and its attendant duties and hardships with joyful submission. The only social relationships which Lutheranism actively sought to penetrate with the new spirit of the gospel were those of the family. In our twentieth century disintegration of family life, it is well for us to remember the profound effect Protestantism has had on civilization for four hundred years by making the family a religious as well as biological and economic community. Those who admire ecclesiastical virginity for its own sake have never been able to forgive Luther's marriage to the ex-nun Katherine. This was not, despite vulgar polemics, another case of Henry VIII and Anne Boleyn, but the result of Luther's tardy conviction that his preaching about the Christian dignity of the married estate would gain force by demonstration. Neither lust nor modern romantic love played a role here, but something deeper than either, the service of God in the role of spouse and parent. Protestantism has discovered that both the prayer and the self-mortification of the monastery can readily permeate family relations and in the mutual ministry of this intimate fellowship in labor and in family worship much of the secret of Protestant strength has lain. Protestantism has also known its celibates "for the sake of the Kingdom," but honors them only for that reason.

It was Calvinism which interpreted the doctrine of vocation in an activist sense, justifying the change of business and of social status, if done not for greed or ambition but for a more ample obedience. "While the passivity and happy surrender of Lutheranism," Troeltsch observed, "combined with its emotional warmth and naivete, with its tendency to give rein to natural impulses, has left its mark, in the form both of a dependent spirit and of geniality, upon large sections of German civilization right down to the present day, the school of Calvin, on the other hand, has bred in the Calvinistic nations a habit of personal reserve, positive restraint, aggressive initiative and a reasoned logic of the aim of action." The "school of Calvin" means not merely the Reformed and Presbyterian churches, but the whole body of what we have called the Puritan tradition. These churches possess a recognizable unity of ethos in their inheritance of a keen interest in politics, but not for the sake of the state, active industry within the economic sphere, but not for the sake of wealth, unceasing labor, ever disciplining the senses, and all originally to glorify God, to produce the Holy Community.

Today this spirit has almost entirely disappeared from the political, economic, and technical institutions which it was instrumental in creating. While democracy of the Anglo-Saxon type and the rationalized structure of modern economic production and technology are historically inconceivable without the contribution of ascetic Protestantism, now they are largely informed by other ideas and other goals. And within the "school of Calvin" doubts have been gathering for two or three generations as to how adequately this largely secularized capitalistic democracy lends itself to the expression of the mutual ministry of reconciliation.

Puritan Political Ethics

Noting the sharp contrast with the patriarchal Lutheran tradition of the Continent, we may properly dwell at more length on the most influential political ethic of the modern world, the Puritan democracy of the English-speaking countries. Liberalism, both in terms of civil liberties and of popular participation in government, was in considerable degree shaped if not created by the Puritans of England and America. To this day Anglo-American liberalism, even in its secularized forms, shows a humanitarian, responsible and freedom-loving aspect little evident in the liberalism of Romanist and Lutheran countries. Liberalism in Holland, England and North America has been significantly Christianized. In Romanist France, Italy, Spain, Latin America, as in Orthodox Russia and Lutheran Germany, political, religious and intellectual liberty has only been won, where it has been won, by co-operation with anti-religious forces against the intolerance and authoritarianism of the clergy. Quite in contrast to the temper of English and American liberals is the resultant bitterness and hostility of the great majority of educated people and political liberals to ecclesiastical Christianity in all these other nations. This continental liberalism, moreover, has tended to be as intolerant as the churches it fought. While the proportion of the American population claiming church membership has steadily increased from a tenth in colonial days to half of the

whole, in France the same proportion in the same years has
dropped from a nominal hundred per cent to less than one
quarter. Latin America and Spain tell much the same story.
The single most important factor in this contrast is the unique
capacity of the Puritan tradition to meet and to mold in
Christian forms the aspiration of the modern nations for
intellectual and political freedom.

We may begin with the issue of civil liberties and the
separation of church and state and then proceed to the topic
of responsible general participation in the democratic process.
We have already noticed that the unique relationship of
church and state in this country, and our conception of religious liberty, are a legacy from Puritanism in the free-
church phase. In contrast to all the authoritarian church-
state systems, Puritanism was gradually persuaded that the
freedom of the church from state control, and of the state
from ecclesiastical control, was healthy, provided community
and state still felt themselves obligated to the fundamental
moralities of Christianity. This was really a return to the
early medieval pattern of the mutual independence of Christian state and Christian church, before Hildebrand began
the theocratic campaign to subdue the state to the church.
Dante had continued to represent the earlier conception, insisting on the direct religious sanction and responsibility of
the Christian ruler. Calvin's Geneva, closely integrated as
it was, saw nothing like the papal attempts at a theocracy.
The constitutional liberties of the state as against the church
organization were honored on principle. The Calvinist knows
that in its own sphere the state might be right and the clergy
wrong. It has happened. Papalism, by contrast, honors such
independence in the state only where the state has forced
its recognition. Yet such a mutual recognition of authority
and responsibility on the part of the administrators of church
and state is the first condition of religious liberty and its
consequences, civil liberties in general.

A whole-hearted acceptance of religious and intellectual liberty presupposes also a second conviction which was effective in the free-church phase of Puritanism but not in the great church-state systems. This was the insight into the provisional character of all formulations of the communion of the Christian fellowship with God in Christ. The pietists and Methodists and the preachers of the American "Great Awakening" all sensed a common experience of God's redeeming work among men despite varying dogmatic traditions. Schleiermacher viewed all creeds and dogmas as crystallizations of such experience in the terms and language of particular past generations. So viewed, official theologies were authorities to guide men to God, but not absolute and infallible definitions. And as we have seen, this insight was simply a development of the general Reformation view of God's continuing self-disclosure in the church.

Modern Romanism, however, has no use for either of these presuppositions of religious and civil liberty. Roman doctrine is asserted to be final and infallible and in no need of reinterpretation. God spoke once and then retired, leaving the papacy as his executor. The papacy, moreover, does not feel wholly free to accomplish its mission until it actually governs governments. Official Romanism will always consider itself "persecuted" until it is free to persecute. This is not true, of course, of the great majority of American Catholic laity, who like the dubiously orthodox Al Smith, are willing to fight for the emancipation of their church, but not for that fuller "freedom" which means servitude and sullen silence for non-Romanists. This they learned, however, not from Rome but from their Protestant neighbors. Rome repudiates freedom of conscience and religion and seeks to muzzle all others while gaining for itself legal and financial establishment by the state. We may comfort ourselves at least with the knowledge that the Roman Court has decided that under present conditions in the world the death penalty

for heresy is not workable. A useful statement of how the
Roman Catholic hierarchy aspires to change the American
constitution eventually may be read from the authoritative
and very widely used text, *Catholic Principles of Politics,*
by Ryan and Boland.* Under a Catholic adjustment of the
Constitution, private worship would be assured to all groups
which should loom no larger than "an insignificant and
ostracized sect." Free speech in pulpit and press, however,
and exemption from taxation would be denied them, for
"error has not the same rights as truth." These proposals
are conceded to be "intolerant, but not therefore unreason-
able," and since "the danger of religious intolerance toward
non-Catholics in the United States is so improbable and so
far in the future, . . . it should not occupy their time or
attention." Wherever the hierarchy gains influence, however, in the schools, in the courts, in municipal politics, in
diplomacy and the state department, in control of the means
of communication, this is its program.

The second aspect of Puritan political ethics, popular
participation in the democratic process, is more elusive. It
is apparent enough, on the face of it, that the democratic
process as understood in America is simply a social and
political application of the dynamic Protestant conception of
the church as the mutual ministry of believers. It is equally
apparent that the whole structure of our government is a
political equivalent of the Calvinist and conciliarist pattern
of a graduated system of representative legislative bodies.
Having observed these striking parallels, however, it is much
more difficult to establish the actual relations between the
spirit and form of church and state, either historically or in
present practice.

The evidence seems, however, to warrant some confidence
that there is a significant carry-over from the religious to the

---

* New York, Macmillan, 1940, pp. 313-321.

political community. This was more evident in the Reformation epoch and the generations immediately following than it is now, for then the various "secular" aspects of life were more vividly measured by the standards of Christian obedience than is now the case. Sunday by Sunday and every day between, it was laid on the consciences of individual members of the Calvinist and Puritan tradition that they were personally responsible for the political conduct of the states of which they were citizens. This is a very different teaching from the paternalism enjoined by ecclesiastically minded Romanists, Anglicans, Lutherans and Orthodox. There it was a matter of submission to the duly constituted authorities, never of personal responsibility for the ethical character of their policies. Romanists, to be sure, were willing to urge resistance to political absolutism, but only in the name and under orders of Roman absolutism. No other religious tradition has systematically trained whole peoples to a sense of their individual and inalienable moral responsibility for the acts of their government.

The mutuality, the tolerance and trust, the give and take of the democratic process is similarly related to the life of the Protestant religious fellowship. It is the democratic conviction that policy is best determined by the conversation and debate of all the several constituent members of the community, each forming and changing his judgment freely and responsibly in the light of his moral obligations. The balance and efficiency of this process are impeded in proportion as members of the political community are denied this responsible participation, as in the case of members of the communist party, or Roman Catholics. In political decisions of various types, more comprehensive for communists than for Romanists, their followers are denied freedom of discussion or decision and sent to vote under orders. On a wide range of issues, such as educational policy on local, state, and national levels, questions of social health and morals involved

in birth control, marriage and divorce legislation, questions
of the immunity of the Roman clergy and property from
civil law, and many issues of foreign policy, the Roman
Catholic citizen withdraws from the democratic process. His
vote is cast under penalty of church discipline by politicians
of the hierarchy who do not submit their purposes or criteria
to public discussion. These policies naturally ramify out into
alliances with specific political machines, or punitive meas-
ures against specific independent legislators, and the last implications may be remote indeed. Educated Romanists, to
be sure, tend to treasure the independence of their political
decisions, but the masses perforce take the priests' opinion
as to when Roman morals or interests are involved in political questions. The case of American policy toward Franco
Spain, for example, seemed to indicate that Catholic voters
as a whole, despite their better judgment as shown by the
Gallup poll, can be brought to heel on the crucial issues by
the unanimous weight of the hierarchy. Like Caiaphas, the
democratic Romanist layman sadly toes the party line. And
this method of controlling democratic procedures by a disciplined undemocratic minority, made familiar by Nazis and
communists, is widely effective also in all sorts of community
and social enterprises into which Catholics enter.

A significant, if involuntary, compliment to the superior
virility of Puritan political ethics has been paid by the Roman
church in this last generation. Becoming increasingly unsure
of its position in the countries where it has had a free hand
to train peoples to Christian citizenship, the Roman hierarchy
has apparently recently decided to transfer its political base
to the nations whose common life is still most effectively
regulated by Christian morality, the English-speaking peoples. A great concentration of personnel and other resources
has consequently been devoted in this generation to establish
a new home in Britain and America for the church which
has so signally failed to teach political ethics to southern and

central Europe and to South America. Now American Roman Catholics have proved their loyalty to this country in all her wars. They have not been demonstrated to be more susceptible to political corruption than non-Catholics, other factors being equal. One may, nevertheless, doubt whether they will or can contribute their proportionate share to American democracy. Roman Catholic democrats are concerned about this weakness, but the cause lies in the very heart of the system. An absolutism can train solid, loyal, efficient, law-abiding citizens, but it cannot train them to be *free;* it cannot produce responsible initiative in each individual layman. Romanism could never have created the Anglo-Saxon type of democracy and it is unlikely to contribute its share toward its maintenance.

Yet the heirs of the Puritans have no grounds for complacency. Much of the history of the last two hundred and fifty years has been a record of the increasing retrenchment and impoverishment of the Protestant ethic. We have mentioned certain contributing factors.* Nevertheless the results are disturbing. Business and politics in particular were very widely declared out of bounds for the Christian conscience and the Christian was recommended to "save his soul" as an individual and to be "religious" in one carefully insulated department of his mind and heart. Thus Protestantism has notably regressed to the medieval conception of "the religious" life as a segregated life of pietistic emotion and thought. Those scattered Protestants who have insisted on the full sovereignty of God over all activities of the community in the Reformation tradition have been lately stigmatized as "religious socialists" and not quite nice. The tide is unmistakably turning, to be sure, but the recovery of an evangelical ethic will be an arduous struggle. Everywhere over the Protestant world, however, there are springing to

---

* cf. pages 80 and following.

light little groups and cells and communities of those
quickened by the eternal gospel and determined to build a
new fellowship with an ethic related to every aspect of life
in society. Protestantism is in revolution because the evangelical movement is again on the march.

The Motive and Hope of Christians

In a deeper sense than Bossuet understood, revolution is
the proper state for the evangelical community. The Protestant vocation can never finally be defined in terms of any
institution or program, monarchical, parliamentary, capitalistic, socialistic, although every generation must make its
responsible decisions for some such structure and Protestants
have championed all of these. Nor will Protestantism ever
rival the ecclesiastical machinery and bureaucracy of the
sacrosanct institutions. The role of the Protestant institution
is to preserve the gospel which calls every institution to
judgment, and the Protestant church has done its duty if it
has brought down on itself the truly evangelical criticism of
its children. In a day of insecurity and widespread yearning
for authority, Protestantism is no doubt at some disadvan-
tage. Yet if Protestantism is defensive about its established
position and practices, it becomes an *ersatz* Catholicism and
loses its reason for existence. Protestantism can only save its
life by losing it. All securities and institutions must be re-
linquished before the one security, the will of the living
God speaking through the mutual ministry of believers. As
Richard Niebuhr wrote of the Puritans who came to New
England, "What they did not foresee was that the positive
part of church reformation was not a structure, but a life, a
movement, which could never come to rest again in secure
habitations, but needed to go on and on from camp to camp
to its meeting with the evercoming Kingdom."

Like the Marxist, the Christian knows of a power at work

in history independent of his desires or even his existence, but to which he may become associated, and in which he may find his fulfilment. Unlike the Marxist, however, the Christian may commune directly with this power, and discover in it a solicitation for himself apart from his role as a unit in class and national struggles. The most orthodox socialist, democrat, capitalist or pacifist may also be personally unstable and anti-social and none of these programs answers the ultimate problem of individual life. For the short term such political religions seem more effective than Christianity, which can never seem to state clearly and simply whether it is socialist, capitalist, pacifist, democratic. And just for that reason the political religion must be ruthless. As the Marxist said to the Christian "We are more desperate than you, for we have but this once. If we fail now, we fail forever. You can fail and fail and yet succeed."

The bond of Christian fellowship cuts deeper and lasts longer than any ethical program because it assumes the inadequacy and evil in every ethical program in which Christians are engaged. Christian soldiers can even fight each other with a deep sense of fellowship, as lovers forgive in each other their mutual exploitation or as parents and children, employers and employees perceive and forgive in each other their lust to domination and self-assertion. For Christians have a hope which cannot be dashed by the perishing of any specific state or civilization or reform. In a time of the breaking of nations it is hard to see what other hope than this can endure, save the hope of death and oblivion. The Christian expects something less than social or political or economic success, and something vastly more, a fulfilment and transfiguration of his fragmentary and halting obedience in the life of God himself. Yet this resurrection and transfiguration will be of the "body," that is, of the concrete personality in all its social and historical relations.

The Christian's hope is thus implicit in his first confession before the figure of Jesus Christ: "My Lord and my God!" The recognition that in Jesus Christ there is more than superlative goodness, that there is also ultimate *power*, is at the same time the recognition that the destroyer and creator of nature, the exuberant energies of the universe, are ultimately Christlike, and *good*. The God of nature is not in the last analysis as D. H. Lawrence or Robinson Jeffers sees him, beautiful and cruel and careless, but the Father of our Lord Jesus Christ. Thus it is first from our redemption that we understand the creation and our place in the world of things. God has scattered hints of himself everywhere, in "the starry sky above and the moral law within," and has permitted man the means of an imposing accumulation of useful science, but for a certain and saving knowledge of the significance of our lives and their proper orientation we must turn to the particular revelation in history of Jesus his Messiah. As our personal decisions are shaped in personal relations with the community of believers and Christ its head, so we perceive these qualities and relations to be the most determinative factors in the universe, the crucial revelatory moments of the intention and meaning of the whole continuous creative process of the cosmos. In the degree that the Christian puts his faith in Christ, he dares to trust the unknown God. He is assured that while many of God's ways will remain incomprehensible to him, nevertheless, in Christ he has the full and adequate presentation of God's nature and purpose so far as mortality is capable of it.

While we may feel with Luther, that the "Trinity" is an inappropriately mathematical term for God, we discover its essential meaning implicit in the good news of the historical revelation. We know that no spirit is the Holy Spirit which is not also the Spirit of Jesus Christ, and we know that all we can comprehend of the hidden Father is fully disclosed in Jesus Christ. And knowing that the Eternal bears Jesus Christ risen in glory in his unending life we can dare to hope also for everlasting life in him. Thus it is that to the three major ventures of the church's oldest confession of faith is added the audacious Christian hope:

I believe in God the Father Almighty, maker of heaven and earth, . . .
and in Jesus Christ, his only son, our Lord . . .
in the Holy Spirit, the holy church catholic, the communion of saints, the forgiveness of sins, . . .
the resurrection of the body, and the life everlasting. Amen.